SCARCE HEARD AMID THE GUNS
John McCrea

The experiences of a Gunner officer in the First World War
as recorded in his diary and letters home

John Potter

Published in 2013 by
Northern Ireland War Memorial
21 Talbot Street Belfast BT1 2LD
www.niwarmemorial.org

ISBN 978-1-909751-02-6

Designed by John McMillan
Printed by Nicholson Bass Ltd. Belfast

Cover Image © Imperial War Museum (Q9347)

Contents

Lieutenant Colonel Claud Furniss Potter CMG DSO

Foreword

I was very pleased when John Potter asked me to write a foreword to his book, as it gave me an early opportunity to read it, which I did with great interest.

The book is essentially an account of one man's war, the author's father, Lieutenant Colonel Claud Furniss Potter CMG DSO, Royal Artillery. The core of the book is provided by Colonel Potter's voluminous diary and the carefully preserved letters which he wrote to his mother. In the diary entries and the letters, Potter holds nothing back, which helps to explain why they are so vivid and immediate. Even the requests for items to be sent to him tell their own story.

In addition, John Potter cleverly uses a variety of sources to present the wider picture of the ten major battles in which his father was involved. But it is the diary and letters which tell of the bravery and hardships suffered by Great War soldiers.

One thing that emerges clearly is that Claud Potter was an energetic and thoughtful regimental officer and a most able staff officer dealing with major operations and difficult situations. He regularly visited his forward troops and even the observation posts which for a time were essential to the artillery. As well as caring about his soldiers, he also looked to the welfare of the many horses which were essential to the gunners.

A particularly poignant chapter in the book deals with the death in action of Claud's younger brother, Ken. He was awarded a DSO following a great act of courage but he did not live to learn about the award.

As anyone who knows him would have expected, John Potter has done an excellent job with this book. I have read quite a few works about the Great War but I believe that this one gives perhaps the most vivid account of the hardships involved for the officers and other ranks, as well as being a useful account of the operation of the artillery in the war. I have no hesitation in recommending it to Gunners in particular, as well as to the general reader.

Colonel John Steele CB OBE TD DL
President, The Royal Artillery Association (NI)

In Flanders Fields

In Flanders fields the poppies grow
Between the crosses, row on row,
That mark our place; and in the sky
The larks, still bravely singing, fly
Scarce heard amid the guns below.

We are the Dead. Short days ago
We lived, felt dawn, saw sunset glow,
Loved and were loved, and now we lie
In Flanders fields.

Take up our quarrel with the foe:
To you from failing hands we throw
The torch; be yours to hold it high.
If ye break faith with us who die
We shall not sleep, though poppies grow
In Flanders fields.

John McCrea
May 1915

Preface

This is not a history of the First World War, rather it is the story of that war as my father experienced it. He was present at every major battle, except the Marne in 1914 and Arras in April 1917. Throughout he kept a diary, filling six hardbacked volumes (extracts from these diaries and letters to his mother are in italics), frequently including sketch maps of his walks to the front line and the location of his batteries. At Cambrai in 2009 I was able to find from one of these sketches hollows in the ground that had been his howitzer battery positions in Havrincourt Wood.

I have also inherited my father-in-law's 1:40,000 map sheet 28 dated January 1918 covering Belgium and part of France, from Poperinghe to Menin. I have included the map references in the text to enable future generations of our family to follow in my father's footsteps. Towns have spread out obliterating places with famous names. Broad new roads have carved up the battlefields, particularly around the north side of Ypres. Yet when peace came in November 1918, the farms were rebuilt on their former sites and the old country roads still follow the same routes. In 2009 I was able to drive straight to the site of the dugout where my father's war ended, using the 1918 map. I was surprised to find how easy it was to find my way round around the battlefield using a map surveyed 95 years ago.

Like most veterans, Claud never talked to us about the war and we, sensing his reluctance, never questioned him about it. It is something I much regret.

I must record the names of a number of people who helped and advised me in putting together this account. Richard Doherty, a prolific military historian and an old friend, read the original draft and advised me to submit it for publication. What makes the account unusual, he pointed out, is that it covers the experiences of a regular army officer who served almost from the start to the end of the war in two separate capacities, as a divisional staff officer and as an artillery brigade commander. John Hughes proof read the typescript. John McMillan undertook the design of the book. My son Tony typed the script and provided the photographs of places my father would have known, as well as suggesting the title for this book. Terence Nelson, custodian of the Royal Ulster Rifles Museum, helped my research by allowing me access to the museum library. I am also most grateful to the Northern Ireland War Memorial, which supported the publication of this book.

The largest debt I owe is to an old lady, my grandmother, whom I never knew. She kept every letter which her two sons wrote from the battlefield, carefully preserved in their original envelopes. There are about 170 of them. They provide an intimate and remarkably open account of what life was like at the front.

John Potter

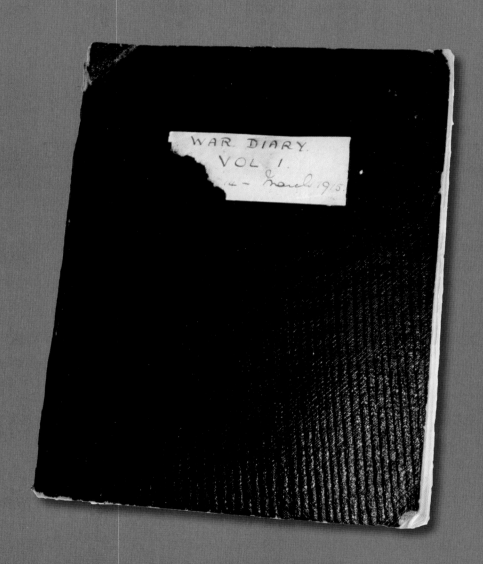

WAR DIARY.
VOL I.
14 – March 1915

Chapter 1   JOURNEY TO THE FRONT
18 September – 27 October 1914

On 2 August 1914 the German army crossed the frontier into Belgium. Two days later, the day after the annual bank holiday, the British government declared war. At that time my father, Claud Furniss Potter, was home on leave from India. Commissioned from the Royal Military Academy (the 'Shop') in the first week of the new century, he had served for six months in South Africa in the last stages of the Boer war. After two happy years soldiering in Kilkenny, he had gone out to India in July 1904.

Claud attended the Staff College in Quetta in 1912/13, passing out top of his year. He was posted as battery captain to 28 Battery Royal Field Artillery, a unit of 7th (Meerut) Indian Division, stationed in Meerut.[1] He was 31 years old, being born on 26 May 1881. It was the first time he had come home from India in ten years. Under the newly published 1912 leave regulations, he was entitled to two years' home leave on completion of ten years' Indian service. It must have been a sad homecoming. His father, William Furniss, had died in 1907.

---

[1] As a result of the Indian Mutiny in 1857 the Governor General advised the House of Commons that "*in no way in future should the natives of the country be entrusted with British Artillery, nor should any native in India be instructed in the use of such dangerous weapons. The native drivers are good horsemen and the gunners most excellent; and in proportion as they are most valuable to the governments they serve, so are they most formidable when they choose to be rebellious.*" Mountain and Field units on the North West Frontier continued to be manned by native gunners, but thereafter all other artillery units were British, and continued to be so until 1938. *History of the Regiment of Artillery, Indian Army*, Edited by Major General D K Palit, p.31.

His widowed mother had sold the family home in Ilkley, 'Arundel Lodge', built by his father William in the 1880s, and moved to Bickley in Kent to be nearer her parents in Angmering in Sussex. Her father was proprietor of the West Sussex Gazette and had served several terms as Mayor of Arundel.

The Indian army of 1914 was not prepared for a major war outside India. Although it was supposed to provide up to two divisions for overseas expeditions, no forces had been specifically earmarked or organised for that purpose. Nevertheless, on 8 August two infantry divisions, 3rd (Lahore) and 7th (Meerut), and the 7th (Secunderabad) Cavalry Brigade were mobilised. Within two weeks the Lahore Division had sailed from Karachi and Bombay, landing at Marseilles from 26 September[2]. The departure of the Meerut Division was delayed almost a month by the presence of the German light cruiser *Emden* in the Indian Ocean.

While Claud waited at home for orders to return to his battery, the British Expeditionary Force (BEF) had been engaged alongside the French in bloody and exceedingly costly battles to stem the German advance. On 6 August the War Cabinet had authorised the despatch of four infantry divisions and one cavalry division, made up of the regular army units reinforced with reservists, former soldiers recalled to the colours, many of whom had battle experience from the Boer War. They disembarked at Le Havre and moved in trains to a concentration area between Le Cateau and Mauberge. They numbered one hundred thousand. Despite the Kaiser's disparaging order of the day referring to them as a "contemptible little army", in many respects the BEF was the best organised, best trained and best equipped force that the British had ever sent to war. They had the advantage over both the Germans and the French in being composed entirely of regular and ex-regular soldiers.

On 20 August the divisions set out on the 20 mile march into Belgium in warm, sultry weather. Three days later they had taken up positions alongside the French 5th Army on the Mons-Condé Canal.

[2] *The Indian Army*, Boris Mollo, p. 139. These Indian formations were the first troops from the Empire to enter the field of battle. In all India provided 1,440,500 men, over twice as many as Canada which provided the highest total from the Dominions. *The Imperial War Museum Book of the Western Front*, Malcolm Brown.

The German battle plan, the Schlieffen Plan, drawn up in 1905 by the Chief of the General Staff, was based on an advance through Belgium heading for Paris, with the aim of encircling the capital and trapping the French force between there and the German armies massed on the Franco-German border. By 23 August their advance had reached the Mons-Condé canal. The BEF, in action for the first time, put up a spirited resistance, but was forced to conduct a fighting retreat the following morning. The BEF was in danger of being outflanked on its right by the withdrawal of the French 5th Army, whilst on its left there were only a few French territorial units and detachments of cavalry between its flank and the English Channel. By the time the retreat was halted, the BEF had fallen back to within 15 miles of Paris, having marched 200 miles in 13 days. Units were completely exhausted. At least 15,000 soldiers had been lost, killed, wounded or missing. The artillery had lost 42 guns, 38 at Le Cateau. The German army was equally exhausted, their supplies of ammunition and food running low, and facing an acute shortage of experienced officers and NCOs to replace battle casualties.

At that stage the Germans made a mistake which, if the Allies had reacted with more speed and greater resolution, might have brought the war to an early conclusion. Believing that the French 5th Army and the BEF were exhausted to the point of no longer being fit for battle, Kluck, the German 1st Army commander, turned away from Paris and crossed the French and British fronts to attack the main part of the French force on its left flank. In so doing he exposed his own right flank to counter attack. Seizing the opportunity the Allies returned to the attack with the French 5th Army on the right, the BEF in the centre and on the left the new French 6th Army, reinforced by 6,000 men ferried out of Paris in a fleet of taxis. Over the next six days, in what became known as the Battle of the Marne, the Germans were forced back to the line of the River Aisne. The BEF crossed the river on 12 September and dug in. On 20 and 26 September the Germans launched major counter attacks but were driven off with heavy losses on both sides. With the opposing armies exhausted, the front stabilised as the fighting moved northwards, eventually reaching the Channel coast, with each side trying to turn the flank of the other. Meanwhile, the first troopships bringing the Indian corps began arriving at Marseilles.

4

Claud was staying in the Royal Artillery mess in Aldershot when the telegram arrived ordering him to report to Southampton two days later, on 18 September, to embark for Marseilles on the *Gloucester Castle*, a Union Castle steamer of 8,000 tons.[3] He returned to Bickley to say farewell to his mother. She saw him off at Bromley station. That night he wrote to her, *Keep your pecker up. I shall very soon be back again and quite expect to eat my Christmas dinner with you.*

UNION-CASTLE LINE INTERMEDIATE STEAMER "GLOUCESTER CASTLE."   8,000 TONS.

SOUTHAMPTON – MARSEILLES. *Sept 18th – 26th. 1914.*

Troopship *Gloucester Castle*

Claud spent the night in Ealing with his sister Margie and her husband, Jack Lovatt. The following morning they went with him to Waterloo to see him off on the troop train. He found he had left behind his watch and a bag. Jack took a taxi back to Ealing to retrieve

[3] The liner was later employed as a hospital ship. Whilst evacuating 399 casualties from Gallipoli, she was torpedoed. Almost all the casualties were saved. The ship was salvaged eventually and returned to Britain. In the Second World War she was still in service as a transport, carrying troops between Britain and Cape Town. In July 1942 she disappeared. It was only after the war that it was established that she had been sunk off the coast of West Africa by a German raider, with the loss of 92 passengers and crew.

5

them, returning with minutes to spare. At least this time he had not forgotten his sword, as had happened on a previous occasion.[4]

The *Gloucester Castle* left Southampton that afternoon and sailed to Portsmouth where it anchored for two days, waiting for its escort. That day Claud opened his diary. *At such a moment,* he wrote, *I cannot help but wonder how long a compilation it will be and when I shall be able to write FINIS at the end of it. But one just has to take things as they come, which is after all only a way of saying that one is in the hands of the Supreme Being.*

The troopship finally set sail on 20 September, escorted by an armed merchantman, the *Edinburgh Castle*. To Claud it was a great relief, for he had been worried that he might be ordered ashore at the last moment to fill a staff appointment in one of the headquarters of Kitchener's New Army. Life on board was comfortable. Everyone had cabins. Whisky could be purchased at half a crown a bottle (equivalent to £5.40 in 2013[5]) and Egyptian cigarettes at three shillings for a tin of fifty (£6.50 in 2013). Dinner consisted of four courses.

The other passengers were officers like himself going out to rejoin their units from India, plus 120 members of the Corps of Interpreters being sent out for attachment to the Indian Corps. Most were temporary commissioned officers who had never seen service and who had been drawn from a variety of professions. Some were gentlemen, some not. The one who shared Claud's cabin for the first few nights was drunk regularly and talked in his sleep. They included members of the peerage, journalists, authors, barristers, stockbrokers, etc. One had served in both the British and German cavalry. Another was the son of a friend of Claud's father in Japan. A third was a member of the Mitford family who had recently been the subject of much gossip in the press following his separation under rather painful circumstances from his wife, a daughter of Krupp, the German armaments magnate.

[4] At the beginning of the war officers were armed with a .455 Webley service revolver and a sword. The latter was soon discarded, but there were instances of them being carried into battle, particularly in cavalry charges. Holmes records nine officers in two companies going into the attack on the Aisne in September 1914, "waving their swords as they fell". *Tommy*, Richard Holmes, p.366. Claud still had his sword until the 1950s, when he gave it to a local artillery regiment in Holywood, Co Down.

[5] The National Archives www.nationalarchives.gov.uk/currency.

The voyage was uneventful, warm days and calm seas. Claud gave talks on the artillery and cavalry to the interpreters, whilst they helped him brush up his schoolboy French. He made friends with the ship's black cat and told his mother that he had seen the new moon while on deck and bowed nine times, *so my luck's in*. In the evenings after dinner (*see menu card*) he would listen to the piano playing of one of his fellow passengers, apparently a professional musician. The ship called briefly at Gibraltar where, surprisingly, there were no obvious signs of preparation for war.

On 28 September the *Gloucester Castle* sailed into Marseilles. A fleet of 22 transports had already arrived with the first contingents of the Indian corps. For the next eight days, whilst the troopships disembarked and the corps assembled, Claud's home was a tent in a small camp at St Marcel, eight miles out on the Toulon road. *The Times* special correspondent described the arrival of the Indians in a long, two column article:

"Today it has been my great good fortune to assist at the making of history. I have seen the troops of one of the world's most ancient civilisations set foot for the first time on the shores of Europe. I have seen proud princes of India ride at the head of thousands of soldiers, princes and men alike fired with all the ardour of the East, determined to help win their Emperor's battles or die. And of far greater significance to my fellow countrymen than the making of history, I have seen, welded before my eyes, as it were, what may well prove to be the strongest link in that singular and wonderful link which we call the British Empire."

Dinner menu on board the troopship

"…Hour after hour fully a score of steamers discharged their cargoes, and I am certain happier fighting men never landed in a country where death or glory was to be their goal. Had not the Emperor of India paid them the highest tribute in his Imperial power by asking them to join his white soldiers in crushing the military despotism that was rendering impossible peace and progress in Europe, and therefore upsetting the political balance of the empires and kingdoms of the whole earth. Yes, the King Emperor had done this, and the soul of every Indian of every race represented in that mighty throng was filled to overflowing with a pardonable joy."

"…First came a detachment of stalwart Sikhs, for the greater part head and shoulders above the spectators. Immediately the police guarding the route were swept aside, the ranks were rushed, men and women shook the laughing soldiers by the hand, and young girls showered flowers upon them, pinning roses on their tunics and in their turbans. Tricolours were distributed with prodigality, and it seemed that in a minute or two every second soldier was proudly flying a flag from his rifle. Old ladies with bitter memories of '70 (Franco-Prussian War) pressed forward the better to admire these handsome bearded men with gleaming eyes and flashing white teeth, and it would be difficult to conjure up anything more deeply touching than the sight of those frail women patting the bronze giants on their backs and calling down blessings on their heads."

Claud had reservations about the welcome. *Hear 19 Battery got an extraordinary ovation marching through Marseilles,* he wrote in his diary, *could hardly move for the crowd. Same thing with all native troops. The latter will get hopelessly spoilt. Men and girls shaking hands with sweepers, drabis and syces. A very bad thing having all these troops so near Marseilles. The sooner they get sent off to the front, the better for all concerned.*

For Claud it was an almost idyllic week, the last happy days of the war. The sun shone, it was pleasantly warm, there were reunions with numerous friends he had left behind in India, meeting up in Marseilles for a decent meal. *There is no doubt about our popularity in France. We get a tremendous reception everywhere and everybody. All the children have learnt to say "goodbye" and "goodnight" and every little guttersnipe you meet wants to shake hands.* Claud's French was improving rapidly, though he found it hard to understand the peasants who would lapse into a local patois, whilst he was apt to mix up his French with his Hindustani.

8

Claud (on the left) in camp at St Marcel, near Marseilles

When 19 Battery carried out a drill order, Claud was put in charge of the spectators, amongst them the owner of the land and some very fascinating young ladies. *One little flapper was particularly fascinating and I found I got on splendidly in my French.* The flapper took three photographs and sent copies to Claud.

Monsieur Ambanopula, a Greek Jew, invited Claud and his battery commander to tea at his *château*, a lovely place on top of a hill with a big lake below, fed by a large natural waterfall 100 feet high. A magnificent drive of plane trees all closed at the top reminded him of Savernake forest at Marlborough.

19 Battery, Drill Order, Marseilles. The Battery is still wearing khaki drill and solar topees.

Four of the battery officers were invited to spend a day at the Château de la Reynarde. The ladies of the party all spoke English, two exceptionally well, so they got along splendidly. Another invitation took them to a vineyard where they were shown the processing of the wine, regaled with food and drink and presented with huge baskets of fruit, pears, apples, grapes and figs.

The last peaceful days came to an end on the evening of 8 October when the advance party of the Indian corps left Marseilles to travel by train to Orléans, by way of Toulouse, Limoges, Argentan and Vierzon. The journey took two and a half days. *It was a veritable triumph,* Claud told his mother. *At every place we stopped we were greeted by huge crowds who cheered and clapped and presented us with flowers, fruit, chocolate. All the girls wanted to kiss us and most of us have no buttons left, such was the desire to get souvenirs. Of course our men loved it. (Personally I had no complaints either!) They got free beer, cigarettes, milk and every conceivable luxury. Very charming girls in the centre and west of France*, he recorded in his diary, *and not at all shy. Afraid my allowance of 35 lbs won't allow of me keeping a quarter of my souvenirs, though I swore to keep each one of them à toujours.* At Toulouse some of the officers were taken by car to the Arsenal to look at captured German guns, all very much knocked about by shell fire. *Toulouse a lovely town and looked most beautiful in a fine sunset with a distant view of the Pyrenees from the bridge over the Garonne. There is no doubt about the popularity of the English in France just now.*

The train pulled into Orléans about midnight on 7 October. It was near freezing. The march to camp was most unpleasant, and it was 4.30 am before the officers settled down in their valises fully dressed and warmed by a fire made from scavenged wood.

Three weeks passed whilst the two Indian divisions assembled. At first the weather was fine, even hot, but the nights were bitterly cold. The officers and men were living in tents. Claud asked his mother to send him a parcel of warm clothing, gloves, bed-socks, vests, and 'Long Johns' with legs down to the ankle. In a later letter he asked for a pair of gum boots, and drew a sketch in case his mother did not know what they looked like. He seems to have been ill-prepared for the winter, perhaps lulled by the widely held belief that it "would all be over by Christmas". At last the first mail since he left home had caught up with him, together with copies of the *Daily Mail*, the first opportunity for a long time to catch up with the war news.

The battalions had arrived ill clad for the rigours of a European winter. Arrangements were made to issue warm clothing: the short greatcoats known as 'British Warms', pullovers, balaclavas and 'Long Johns'. These were made with a flap in the seat, allowing the wearer to defecate without lowering his trousers, thus exposing his extremities to the bitter wind. Unfortunately they were not designed for smaller soldiers such as the Gurkhas, and the first task given to the interpreters of 1/9 Gurkha Rifles was to go to the Orléans market and buy three thousand pins.[6]

As the divisions had had to leave behind in India much of their transport, apart from the officers' chargers, the opportunity was taken to requisition from Orléans and the surrounding countryside

---

[6] *Sepoys in the Trenches*, Gordon Corrigan, p. 45.

farm carts, mules and horses, including for each battalion 18 of the heavy draught horses, accustomed to the plough. For the Ghurkhas in particular, they were a handful. "A normally well disciplined smart battalion was reduced to the appearance of a circus, with carts and horses galloping in all directions, totally out of control, with an excited follower or stolid (albeit beginning to worry) Gurkha perched on top of the wagon, trying without the slightest result to control his runaway steed. One overran a staff officer's tent. He was not amused." [7]

Claud had been appointed camp adjutant, an unpleasant job and very hard work. *I had to meet troop trains and escort units to their camps at all times of the day and night, select and allot billets, march out camps and general bottle-washer. Many nights I did not get to bed until 4am. To make matters worse the weather broke and we had a week of pouring rain. The camp a regular morass. I wasn't dry or warm for five days. I'm getting quite good at French now,* he told his mother. *One gets plenty of practice. Not a soul seems to be able to speak any English, even in the shops. Yesterday I went round several of the farms in the neighbourhood to buy milk, eggs, butter and vegetables. Wherever I went I quite enjoyed myself, for I was received with enthusiasm and regaled with wine, fruit, etc. I was very popular in one place because I kissed the baby, a nasty, slobbery little thing it was too. However, one must do all one can for the entente! At another place I kissed a little girl who wasn't quite so young. That I enjoyed more. I'm afraid you will think it is time I got off to the front!* One of his duties was to find billets for the divisional staff. Most of the householders were keen enough to put up officers but there were some sticklers. *My word the French women do chatter. Every house we go to they want to give us a full history of their family affairs and show us all their property from top to bottom of the house. Then one has to make oneself pleasant by kissing the baby and patting the pigs.*

Whilst still in Orléans, Claud suffered two disappointments. On arrival in Marseilles he had learnt that his place in 28 Battery had been filled by another officer in India in his absence. He assumed that it would be a temporary arrangement and that he would be reinstated when the battery caught up with him in Orléans. Now he learnt that his replacement, who was a friend of the battery commander, would remain in the appointment. Claud was left without a battery.

---

[7] Ibid p.43

To offset his disappointment General Scott, Commander Royal Artillery of the Meerut Division, asked for him to be posted to his headquarters as staff captain. The appointment was approved by the divisional commander, General Anderson, and published in divisional orders. Claud had transferred his tent and belongings to the headquarters camp when he learnt that the artillery adviser, Freddy Mercer and Claud's *bête noir*, had had the posting cancelled, ostensibly on the grounds that he could not afford to lose any of his officers to the staff. The real reason, Claud surmised, was that Scott had had the posting agreed without first consulting Mercer, and the two could not stand each other. Left without a job, Claud was afraid he would be appointed OC of 4th Brigade ammunition column. However, the CRA found a place for him in 7 Battery in 4th Brigade. The battery commander was an old friend and *quite a nice fellow if one takes no notice of his liver in the mornings.*

By now most of the Meerut Division had assembled. It was time to move on. *We move off tomorrow (27th October)*, he told his mother. *I confidently expect that we shall be in the thick of things some days before this letter reaches you. It will be splendid to really get started at once, as I am sick of messing about like I have been doing these last five weeks with nothing at all to show for it. It's very late and getting cold. I am writing this at the mess table out in the open with only a candle. It's so damp the paper is like pulp. Goodnight Mother dear. My very best love to you and keep your end up. We've all got to do our little bit now for the old country.*

Chapter 2   **INTO BATTLE**
THE FIRST BATTLE OF YPRES
20 October – 11 November 1914

With stalemate at the centre, both sides looked to the north, the Channel coast and the Flanders plain, each hoping to outflank the other in an area that so far had been only lightly defended. Sir John French, the British Commander-in-Chief, obtained the reluctant agreement of the French to move the BEF from the Aisne to Flanders, shortening his lines of communication to Britain and providing an opportunity, or so he hoped, to open an offensive into Belgium, round the German right flank. The move took place during the first two weeks of October, the infantry travelling by train, the cavalry on horseback, the divisions deploying between Ypres and La Bassée. They were reinforced by 7th Division which had landed at Zeebrugge and taken up positions at Ghent to protect the Belgian army withdrawing from the fortress at Antwerp. When the fortress fell, the division marched south west to take up positions on the BEF's left flank. Later the BEF was reinforced by the Indian Corps and 8th Division, increasing its total strength from 120,000 to nearly 200,000.

Meanwhile the German 4th Army was advancing along the Channel coast and through Belgium, aiming to smash the Allied left flank and capture Calais. When their advance on the port was thwarted by the Belgian engineers opening the flood gates just in time, flooding the Yser, they concentrated their attacks on the environs of Ypres. They entered the town on 13 October but did not stay. The British took it the following day and held it for the rest of the war.

The Flanders countryside was ill-suited for battle. Apart from modest but tactically significant high ground north east, east and south east of Ypres, it was flat land, small fields, still under cultivation that autumn, and divided by high hedges, streams and water-filled ditches. The soil was heavy and glutinous, so that the roads quickly became churned into mud. It was ground where observation over any distance was difficult, and the high water table caused the trenches to flood.

What became known as the First Battle of Ypres opened on 20 October, when the German 4th Army attacked along the whole front. During the next three weeks they made a series of massive attacks, reaching a climax on 31 October when they nearly broke the British line. According to Farndale, it was perhaps the greatest day of crisis ever to face the British army.[8] The German 4th Army outnumbered the BEF two to one, but it was made up mainly of reservists, among them volunteer university students and schoolboys. They did not lack courage. There were reports of them advancing *en masse*, arms linked. But they were no match for the seasoned regular soldiers and reservists of the BEF, trained to fire 15 rounds a minute from their Short Magazine Lee-Enfield rifles, a rate of fire so intense that their opponents assumed they were using machine guns. In fact, at that stage there were only two machine guns per battalion.

Already worn down by two months of fighting at Mons and on the Aisne, the British battalions fought from hastily dug, often shallow trenches and ditches built up with sandbags. There were only rudimentary barbed wire defences constructed from farm fences. There was also an alarming shortage of artillery shells. In October there were only 150 rounds per gun in France.[9] There was little defence in depth, as there were almost no reserves. They occupied the trenches, often flooded, for the full three weeks, without rest, dirty, unshaven, their uniforms reduced to little more than rags. The Germans made one more major attack, on 11 November, and again were driven off. For the Allies it was the end of the crisis. Though attacks continued for another ten days, both sides were played out. Living conditions had become unbearable and snow had begun to fall.

---

[8] *History of the Royal Regiment of Artillery, The Western Front 1914–1918*, General Sir Martin Farndale, p.74.

[9] Farndale, ibid p.73.

The BEF had suffered 58,155 casualties at Ypres. Of the 84 infantry battalions on 1 November, 18 had fewer than 100 men, 30 fewer than 200, 26 fewer than 300, and only 9 exceeded 300. Their total casualties since the first engagement at Mons were 86,237.[10] The pre-war regular army had been destroyed. After the battle few survived, only the memory of its spirit.[11]

The Aisne, and now Ypres, saw the beginning of trench warfare. The trenches stretched from the Channel to the Swiss border, taking a line that was to remain little changed for the two years. Deadlock had set in.

First Ypres had begun without the Indian Corps. When the situation grew desperate, Sir John French brought up the Indian divisions to relieve II Corps in the southern sector near Bethune (the Meerut Division) and to assist I Corps on the Ypres front (the Lahore Division). Wherever they fought they fought hard, but for them it was a harsh war, for which they were neither prepared nor equipped. Despite the efforts to issue the men with limited warmer clothing in Orléans, it was December before there was a general issue of effective winter dress.

Throughout the war the Royal Field Artillery (RFA) was equipped with 18 pounder guns capable of firing up to 18 rounds a minute to a maximum range of 6,500 yards, though this could be increased to 7,800 yards by digging in the trail. Initially the only ammunition available for the field batteries was the shrapnel shell. Valuable for engaging troops in the open, it was of limited use against trenches, dugouts and buildings. Claud's battery fired high explosive shells for the first time on 22 November. Later the ammunition was supplemented with gas, smoke and incendiary projectiles.

The RFA was organised in brigades under the command of a lieutenant colonel. The brigade consisted of three batteries, each commanded by a battery commander (BC) with the rank of

[10] *The Old Contemptibles,* Keith Simpson, pp.108–109

[11] *History of the First World War,* Liddell Hart, p.178

[12] Later a 4.5 inch howitzer battery was included in each brigade. The three brigades that came from India with the Meerut Division were 4th (7, 14 and 66 Batteries); 9th (19, 20 and 28 Batteries) and 13th (2, 8 and 44 Batteries).

major.[12] The battery was sub-divided into three sections, each of two guns, under the command of a subaltern. Each gun was manned by a detachment of six men, with a further four men per gun at rest in the wagon lines, the battery administrative area where the horses were held, meals cooked, and the detachments rotated. Initially the wagon lines were a mile or so behind the gun position; later they were deployed some miles back, out of range of hostile artillery. The battery second-in-command, known as the battery captain (BK), was in charge of the wagon lines. Each gun was towed by a limber (two-wheel carriage) in which the ammunition was carried, drawn by a team of six horses, a driver riding the nearside horse of each pair. The total complement of a battery was five officers and 200 men.[13]

In the South African war the guns had been able to fire only at targets visible from the gun position. In the Russo-Japanese war of 1904–05 the Japanese had developed the technique of indirect fire. The British artillery quickly learnt the lesson. In 1906 with the introduction of the director on the gun position and a dial sight on each gun to keep all six guns on parallel lines, it was now possible to engage targets out of sight of the guns, with observation stations close to the front line, normally manned by one of the subalterns or the BC himself, directing fire at the targets. By no means all artillery officers were convinced of the effectiveness of indirect fire and, as in past wars, the guns on occasions continued to be deployed well forward in sight of their targets. For that reason, the 18 pounders continued to be fitted with bulletproof shields. At Le Cateau in August when the artillery was deployed forward with the infantry, engaging the advancing Germans over open sights, gun positions were overrun, resulting in the loss of 38 guns. Where observation was difficult in flat country such as much of Flanders, or where suitable observation stations (OSs) such as attics and church towers were increasingly destroyed by enemy shellfire, forward observation officers would be positioned with the infantry in the trenches and go out with patrols. At Ypres specially constructed ladders were used for the first time to extend the view into enemy territory. Contact between the OSs and the guns was maintained by field telephone and each OS party included a signaller responsible for running out the line

---

[13] *British Artillery 1914–1919*, Dale Clarke.

and mending it when broken, as happened frequently. It was only towards the end of the war that some field batteries were equipped with wireless.[14]

Initially there was no system of grid references, so that targets had to be indicated by reference to names printed on a map (eg, house 200 yards north of second S in Messines). Gridded maps were only introduced during First Ypres in October 1914. 9th Brigade war diary recorded that the squared maps were reported as very good both for bearings to targets and ranges. The range fired by the guns rarely erred by more than 50 yards. The 24 hour clock had not been introduced, and times were designated ack emma and pip emma using the original version of the phonetic alphabet.

The 4th Brigade including 7 Battery left Orléans at night, entraining in pouring rain. The train travelled across France through Etampes, Versailles, Nantes, Rouen, Abbeville and Calais, arriving at Hazebrouck 36 hours after starting out. It had been an uncomfortable journey, uniforms soaked, the carriages cold and in darkness. From Hazebrouck they marched[15] ten miles to Merville where Claud had his first sleep for 40 hours. The officers were billeted in houses, the men in a saw mill. *Very heavy firing to the East and can see flashes of guns in the sky*. On the following day the brigade marched to a village called Locon, about three miles from the front line and billeted overnight in a farm and outhouses. *It simply poured cats and dogs and we were miserable.* During the night 20 stragglers from 8th Ghurkhas sought shelter in the farm.

The next day, 31 October, saw the climax of the German attack to break through the BEF's line at Gheluvelt, east of Ypres and 20 miles from Richbourg, the village where Claud's battery was about to deploy. It was the day that the Kaiser came to the front to witness for himself the defeat of the "contemptible little army", so certain was he that his seven fresh divisions brought up from the Aisne front would break through the front line of the BEF.

---

[14] When I was on my commissioning course in 1944, we were still instructed on how to lay out line as a back-up to the not wholly reliable radios.

[15] In the case of the artillery, 'marching' meant riding on horseback and in horse drawn wagons.

For the first two days the battery was in reserve, bivouacked close to the village of Richbourg St Vaast, a hamlet in open countryside six miles north east of Bethune on the right flank of the BEF. The boundary with the French XXI Corps ran along La Bassée canal, six miles to the south. A German aeroplane dropped a bomb within yards of the battery lines. About an hour and a half later the battery came under fire for the first time when two shells passed overhead and fell well to the rear. *Suddenly we heard a long singing noise and two large shells came overhead. They dropped about 1,000 yards to our left rear. They were two of the big 'Jack Johnstons'* [16] *which burst with a tremendous report and threw up columns of black smoke. This afternoon we had a shell over the bivouac and towards dusk another German aeroplane passed overhead and dropped some bombs but none of them fell near us. The Major and I went out after lunch to reconnoitre alternative gun positions and we had four of these big shells fall only a few hundred yards short of where we were. The Germans are very careless about the way they drop these big fellows about all over the country.*

Realising that their position had been seen by the Germans, the battery moved the bivouac 500 yards to the rear. Claud found quite a nice billet in a public house, with five very saucy little French girls. *About 8 am 2 German biplanes passed over. Our men did some great sniping at them, well led by the Major. Of course no result but all thoroughly enjoyed themselves! Both sides use aeroplanes largely to locate targets, and our airmen have been doing particularly good work in that line. The French have anti-aircraft guns which they run about on armoured motor lorries. We have been interested today watching them firing at German aircraft. The aeroplanes always seem to get away though I'm told one was brought down this morning after flying all down our line to reconnoitre…I must say our fellows are splendid. They go up all day in any weather and, though daily fired at, bring back most valuable information.* [17] Apart from rifle fire, the only defence against aircraft in each division was a section of pom-poms firing a one pound shell, but they were not very effective. It was only in 1915 that the British artillery introduced anti-aircraft guns.

---

[16] The *Jack Johnston* was a heavy German shell that exploded in a cloud of black smoke. The Tommies chose the name after a famous black heavyweight boxer.

[17] The use of aircraft in warfare was so new that most of the Indian soldiers and many of their officers had never before seen an aeroplane.

At dawn on 2 November the battery took over the gun pits of 66 Battery of 4th Brigade. They were well concealed behind a row of poplars, with good overhead cover, between the two Richbourgs, L'Avoué and St Vaast. Battery HQ was in a comfortable cottage 500 yards behind the guns. From there Claud wrote to his mother under the dateline, *Farmhouse in Firing Line. .... the battery has been busy firing away all morning. Though only some 2,500 yards from the German trenches we can see absolutely nothing as the country is dead flat and intersected with farm houses, hedges and clumps of trees. We have to do all our firing by sending out an observation officer right to the front who sends back his observations by telephone. It isn't a pleasant job at all, as he is only about 500 yards away from the Germans. Gage, one of the subalterns, is out this morning. He found his station destroyed on arrival and had to find another, out of which he was shelled in a few minutes. I am at Battery Headquarters... where we have the telephone exchange. We are in communication with the OC Brigade, the gun line and the observation officer, and the actual tactical handling of the battery takes place from here. Things are fairly quiet today, though the infantry have a pretty rotten time.*

The battery was supporting the Garhwal Brigade, made up of the 1st and 2nd Battalions 39th Garhwal Rifles, 2nd Battalion 3rd Ghurkha Rifles and 2nd Battalion The Leicestershire Regiment.[11] *The Germans attack every night and the trenches in some places are only 200 or 300 yards apart. The native troops have been severely tried but they have done awfully well. The guns don't get much attention paid to them but we had 3 of those big 'Black Marias' over about half an hour ago. They fell in a village a few hundred yards to our left rear which is entirely deserted (Richbourg St Vaast). I went through the place yesterday. It is a regular heap of ruins, though 2 or 3 houses are still habitable. One does feel awfully sorry for the poor inhabitants. They have practically nothing to eat, no work to do and every minute are in considerable danger from shells. On the other hand many of them are spies and only stay behind for that reason. They have caught a large number of apparently peaceful*

---

[11] The commanding officer of the Leicesters was Lieutenant Colonel Charles Blackader, an old friend of Claud's from their days in Belgaum. Later promoted to Brigadier, he was given the unenviable appointment of President of the Court Martial which tried and sentenced to death 7 of the 14 leaders of the Easter Rising in Dublin in 1916. He was appointed to command a division in July of that year and died in 1921, having contracted rabies from his pet dog in 1918.

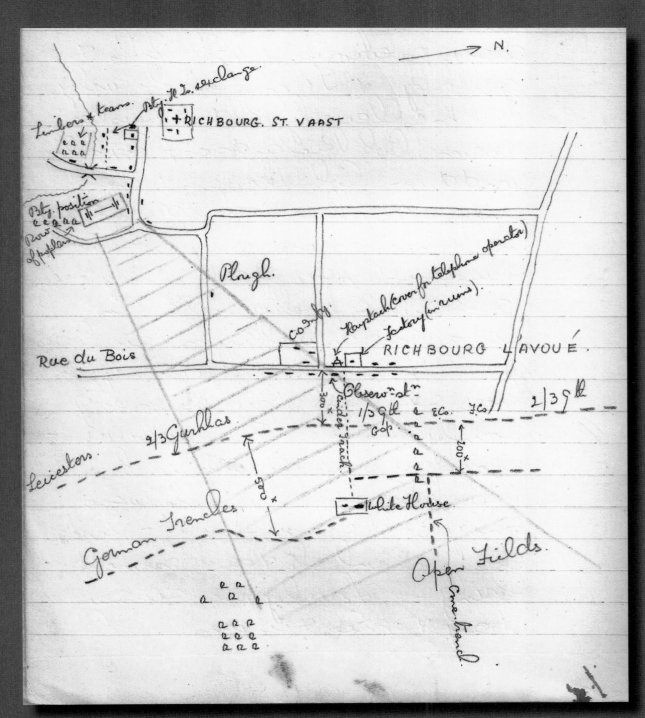

Claud's sketch map of his gun position at Richbourg St Vaast on Monday 2 November 1914

inhabitants signalling to the enemy by fires, smoke from chimneys, lamps, etc. Needless to say they get no mercy.[12]

After dark on the second day at Richbourg, Claud and his subaltern Gage were up in the observation station when the Germans mounted an attack on the 2/39th Garhwalls. *We had the range nicely and gave them about ten rounds of gunfire, being on to them in less than a minute. Attack failed completely and I think we may claim to have been largely instrumental in the result.* He described the observation station to his mother. *It is a house, or as much as is left of it, only just behind our own trenches. In the second storey is a large hole made by a German shell and by cautiously creeping forward and looking through the hole, one can look right down on the German trenches and see them digging and moving about. It isn't safe to put one's head up as the range is only about 600 yards and they have men with glasses on the look-out and as soon as they see a movement 'whiz' goes a bullet. Moreover they shell the building pretty regularly about three times a day. This particular building is the only one left standing of a collection of about 15 or 20. There's practically nothing left of them. Getting to the observation station is no joke either, as there are several open spaces where one invariably gets sniped as one crosses.*

The rest of their first week in action passed relatively quietly, with the battery, constrained by the acute shortage of shells across the whole British front, firing an average of 60 rounds a day, as the Germans continued to mount attacks against the Garhwals. *All these attacks seem to be a bit half-hearted. I hear they are chiefly old men and boys. Probably only Landwehr. A chance shell had killed a sepoy of the Mule Company. He was literally blown to pieces and beside him were 2 horses,*

---

[12] Both amongst the civilian population at home and the soldiers at the front, there was an obsession about spies, and undoubtedly dozens of innocent Belgian and French civilians were shot on unfounded suspicion of spying. However, Claud does record that two British officers had been shot behind the trenches at Richbourg by a German dressed as a sepoy. *Luckily they shot the dirty swine at once. The Germans seem to have no morals as regards the laws and usages of war. There have been several cases of shooting of our fellows right in the rear of our lines by men in civilian dress or in ours or French uniforms. At night they lie up in houses and snipe. Many, I regret to say, prove to be Frenchmen in German pay.* No doubt the accusation is exaggerated. After their defeat in the Franco-Prussian war, the French had no love for the Germans. In any case any passage of information across the two front lines by numerous spies, seems highly improbable.

© Tony Potter 2009

Photograph taken in 2007 looking north west at the gun positions at Richbourg St Vaast. Note the remains of a dugout to the right.

2 mules and all that was left of a mule cart. On the 10 November he wrote to his mother *from the actual gun position sitting in my little funkpit just behind No 1 gun, so this is really a letter from the firing line.* He had had a bath, the first time he had had his clothes off for 15 days. *I was getting right fruity!* He had been suffering from neuralgia and acute toothache and had cycled six miles into Bethune over roads covered in mud and into the teeth of a gale in search of a dentist, but to no avail as they had all departed after the shelling of the town three days earlier. He complained that he had not received *The Times* for about three weeks, *which is very disappointing as one does so want to get news. You see we hear absolutely nothing now. We don't even know what goes on in the batteries and regiments on our right and left.* He concluded with a further list of items he asked his mother to send him: two writing pads, matches in a little tin box, some small pieces of plain chocolate, a small case of coloured chalks, a small camp looking-glass, an India rubber in a small case,[13] a packet of paper (*my Bromo has run out*) and a quite cheap electric torch, a cylindrical shaped thing with a button at the end for providing the current. He explained that all the items needed to be small, as he had to carry them with him.

---

[13] The India rubber in its case is in my desk in 2013.

22

On 5 November 9th Brigade sustained its first casualties. The BC of 28 Battery, Major E H Phillips, and a party of three men who had been observing from a haystack south west of Epinette, had just moved out and were on their way back to the battery when a HE shell struck the road near them. Two men were killed outright. Major Phillips and a fourth member were severely wounded. Phillips died the following day and was buried at Bethune cemetery[14]. He was the BC who in Marseilles had declined to accept Claud back in his former battery. Typically Claud bore him no malice. *He was one of the bravest men I have ever met.*

A long list of promotions had just been published in the London Gazette: some 60 majors, 230 captains and 300 subalterns, mainly to fill appointments in Kitchener's New Army. Claud's name was among the promotions to major. To his delight he was posted in command of 28 Battery, the battery in which he had served in India, to fill the vacancy created by Major Phillips' death. He took over on 14 November. He was glad to leave 4th Brigade. The battery commander of 7 Battery had been an *awfully cantankerous little blighter and, as for the Brigade Commander, he was quite impossible. I fancy he'll end up in a madhouse!*

On the previous night 7 Battery had fired 250 rounds in support of a raid mounted by troops drawn from the Garhwal Brigade. Five days earlier a smaller raid had been successful, catching the enemy unaware. This time the Germans were waiting for them, opening fire with machine guns and artillery, using searchlights to illuminate the battlefield. To make matters worse the shells from the British howitzers were falling short amongst the Garhwalis, who were forced to retire, having achieved nothing at heavy cost. Nine officers and 100 men had been killed.[15]

---

[14] 4 Artillery Brigade war diary, National Archive WO 95/3936. Phillips had served extensively in Africa: on operations in Sierra Leone 1898–99; North Nigeria with Kaduna Expedition in 1908 when he was twice slightly wounded and mentioned in despatches; in West Africa on operations in Ashanti, present at the relief of Dumasi, severely wounded and awarded the DSO; slightly wounded in the Boer War.

[15] For centuries British officers in India had been in the forefront of every battle, leading native troops who had absolute faith in them, no less now than in previous wars. As a result casualties amongst officers in the Indian Corps in France were heavy.

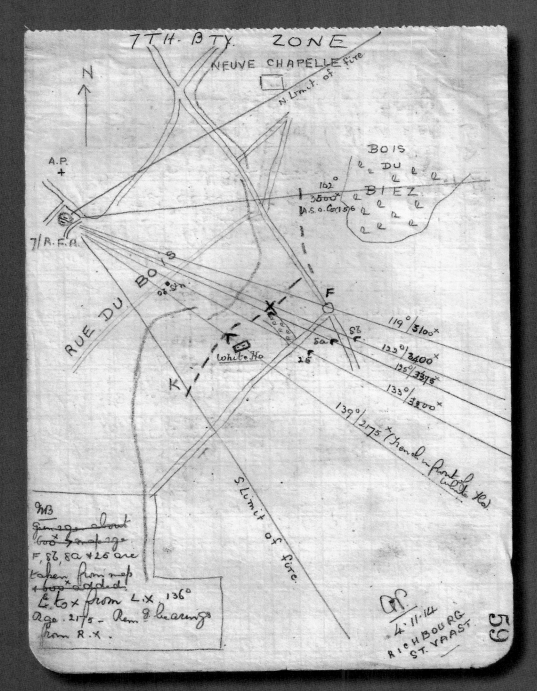

7 Battery Zone, Richbourg St Vaast. Drawn by Claud on 4 November 1914

Chapter 3   WINTER 1914–1915

The Germans made one more attempt to break through the BEF's defences on 11 November, mounting a major attack again in the Gheluvelt sector. The attack failed thanks to the gallantry of the depleted infantry battalions and the devastating fire of the guns. Two German Guards regiments lost 30 officers and 1,300 men, largely due to the accurate fire of one artillery brigade. Though lesser attacks continued until the end of the month, the Germans had abandoned all hope of mounting an offensive in 1914. There were isolated flare-ups along the whole front, in one of which at Festubert Claud was involved, but ammunition was running short on both sides and fighting was largely reduced to persistent sniper fire.

Both sides had come to realise that, given sufficient time and materials to strengthen trench systems, it must become increasingly difficult to break through their enemy's defences. Orders were given that trenches must be dug deeper and approaches covered by barbed wire, but the British lacked entrenching tools. The Germans were better equipped. They had expected to encounter heavily defended strong points, such as the French and Belgian fortresses that had been in the path of their original advance, and so had been equipped with appropriate weaponry, such as trench mortars, demolition charges, and mining and tunnelling equipment. In contrast, the British, in the words of an official historian, were "quite unprepared and had to improvise. Hand grenades were made of jam jars and mortars of field gun cartridges."[16] It was all very well to say "dig deeper", but the high water table of the Flanders fields meant that trenches quickly filled with water from ankle to knee deep. Claud, visiting the infantry entrenched in front of his gun position in his gum boots newly arrived from his mother, found the water was deeper than the boots. He sent another urgent plea for *oilskins, for mackintoshes are useless in the rain such as one gets out here.* Pumps were issued in an attempt to control the water level.

The 1st Battalion The Royal Irish Fusiliers (the 'Faughs') claimed to have invented duckboards, enabling the soldiers to sleep out of the water and using straw purloined from haystacks as beds. Wood from farm buildings and felled trees was used for riveting and for roofing dugouts. In many areas where it was impossible to dig deeper, parapets were built up along the tops of trenches to give greater cover. Primitive periscopes were introduced to thwart the snipers. Back home the women were encouraged to knit pullovers, socks and mittens for their men at the front. Whale oil was issued to combat frostbite and there was a limited issue of leather and goats-fleece lined jackets. Sergeant Wilson of the Faughs recorded in his diary that "It is not uncommon to catch the sentries standing up on top of the parapet hoping to get shot, they felt that miserable".[17] It was a winter that won a reputation amongst the fighting troops as being cursed with above average rainfall.

Despite the fact that the intensity of the fighting had died down, Claud's diary frequently records news of the death or wounding of friends from the Indian years when soldiering was fun, big game hunting, pig-sticking, gymkhanas, polo, picnics, summers in the hill stations, and war was no more than a distant possibility. One such friend was Captain Gray-Buchanan of Ettrickdale on Bute, killed whilst serving with 8th Gurkhas. They had been together at Quetta. He was one of Claud's greatest friends. He had last seen him four months earlier when he was setting out on his honeymoon. The 8th Gurkhas had been involved in very heavy fighting and had lost almost all their original officers.

---

[16] *Imperial War Museum Book of the Western Front*, Malcolm Brown, p.47.

[17] *Angels and Heroes. The Story of a Machine Gunner with The Royal Irish Fusiliers August 1914 to April 1915, as recorded by Sergeant Hugh Wilson MM*, Moreno and Truesdale, p.82.

When Claud took over his new battery, it was deployed at Le Touret, a hamlet four miles south west of Richbourg on the road to Bethune. That same evening a German heavy gun opened fire on the battery. It was nowhere near its target, but when it opened fire again before daylight on the following morning, with 30 to 40 rounds in a 30 minute period, some of the shrapnel exploded above the gun position. The detachments had taken shelter in their pits and the only casualty was the battery megaphone, decapitated by a fragment of shrapnel. Two mornings later, having been able to locate the position of the hostile guns from their muzzle flashes, the battery engaged and silenced them. The war diary records the location as "above the U of Rue in Quinque Rue", one of the last times this antiquated method of target identification was used before the introduction of gridded maps a few days later. That same day the war diary records that "the howitzers of 65 Howitzer Battery, which had come under command of the brigade at the beginning of the month, fired at a German observer who was using a ladder to climb up the wrong side of a haystack, the side clearly visible to the gunners!"

For the first week of Claud's command there was little further enemy activity. For three successive days the battery did not fire a round. As buildings were destroyed by shell fire, it was becoming increasingly difficult to find suitable observation stations. The few that could be used came under persistent attention from snipers. Claud told his mother, *I've been doing a good deal of observing which means going into houses quite close to the German lines. It's quite an exciting game as one invariably gets sniped and very often shelled too. On such occasions one has to rapidly retire from the top storey to the cellar (if there is one) with as much dignity as possible. One does feel sorry for the wretched inhabitants. They are all turned out of the houses, many of which are in ruins. In a village called Richbourg L'Avoué near here, which the Germans shell every day, there literally isn't a house standing with four walls. In many of the houses, especially those in which the Germans have been billeted, every single thing has been ransacked by persons in search of loot. In a house which I was in yesterday observing fire, there wasn't a cupboard or drawer that hadn't been emptied on the floor. Strewn about the place were babies' toys, linen, clothing, broken wine bottles, books and there was actually a large packet of old letters most of them dated 1861. Evidently they were some old treasured letters of the occupants,*

Daily Mail photograph of Festubert. The house on the left is where Claud and his BSM took cover from shellfire. The annotations are by Claud.

probably some love letters. It must be pure wantonness that prompts people to destroy and ransack such things. One sees cows wandering about close to the trenches. A very large number get killed by shell fire, a fate that will eventually overtake all those who do not die of privation, I suppose.

Apart from areas which had been extensively fought over or heavily shelled, the landscape looked remarkably peaceful. Local people still lived near the front line and farming was frequently carried on within the range of the guns. One morning Claud and his BSM had visited the Jats' trenches. Several mortar bombs had fallen close to them, *most horrible things that burst with a tremendous report and are decidedly nasty.* On their way walking to the battery position, they did a detour to look at their observation station in the school house in Festubert. *Germans started shelling with Little Willies as we got into main street. Several fell all around, bringing down all sorts of stuff.*

We got behind a dilapidated house for a while where we felt safe (though we weren't really) and did not get damaged, though a brick discharged from some house fell on my shoulder. Out of about twenty fired, at least ten must have been blinds. That same day a German biplane that had run out of petrol and the engine frozen, landed close to the wagon lines where the pilot was gallantly captured by the padre, though several others claimed the prize. He had with him a large bundle of 'tracts' written in atrociously bad Hindi calling on all Musselmans not to fight against Germany who was befriending the sacred Turks. Since the average Musselman could not read Hindi, the leaflets can have had little effect.

On 22 November [18] Claud, along with one of his subalterns and the BSM, occupied a temporary observation station in the Garhwal Brigade trenches, reeling out a telephone line as they went forward. After careful registration of the zone, bringing the ranging rounds of the gun back to within 60 yards of their own front line, Claud then used the new high explosive shells to target a house reported as containing a nest of snipers. *Number 1 gun did 19 rounds of some of the prettiest shooting I ever saw, practically every round going plump into the house.* The greater part of the house was destroyed and the sniping ceased.

Over the next two days the Indian Corps was involved in its first solo action. For the battery it was its heaviest engagement in the war so far. When that morning Claud went forward to the trenches, he found that the Germans, supported by trench mortars, were carrying out a determined attack, penetrating the line and occupying the trenches on his right. *I now have a pretty good experience of being under heavy rifle fire. At one time things looked pretty nasty and one could get no news as to what was really happening. However, artillery fire prevented them bringing up reinforcements and they were unable to press their advantage.* Claud returned to the gun position under heavy rifle fire. That afternoon the battery fired 250 rounds in support of a counter attack which failed, apparently through hopeless mismanagement.

In the early hours of the following morning, another counterattack mounted by the 39th Garhwalis was highly successful, recovering the lost trenches and taking over some of the enemy's, along with

---

[18] From 20 to 30 November the battery war diary is in Claud's handwriting.

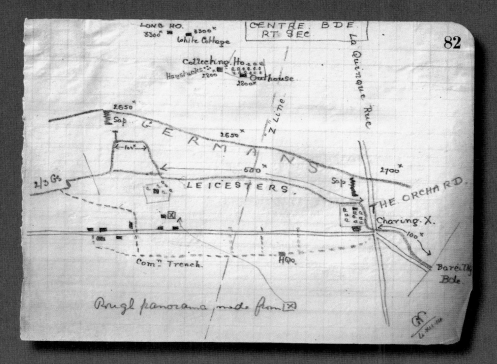

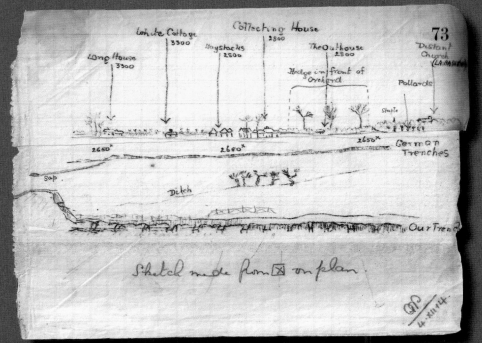

Sketch and panorama
of front line drawn on
4 December 1914

200 prisoners and a trench mortar. The success of the attack was largely due to the gallantry of a sapper officer who led the assault, bombing the Germans from trench to trench, cutting off those who had occupied the British trenches and forcing them to surrender.

The following day, 25 November, the battery was relieved by 81 Battery newly arrived from India, and marched back to a rest area at Robecq, 11 miles to the north west. The billets were bad and the horses out in the open, but at least the men were able to get a decent night's sleep, a change of clothing and an occasional bath. It was their first rest since going into the line 26 days ago. At last Claud was able to have his painful tooth extracted at the field hospital in Merville. He and a companion walked the three miles to St Venant, where they visited a café and were befriended by a Monsieur Flament who took them home and gave them a meal, accompanied by champagne, liqueurs and cigars. Next day, after attending church in Robecq, they returned to the village and were again invited to lunch with Monsieur Flament. *Gave us a slap-up meal with every conceivable form of drink. Got home at 3.30 pm (I think)!*

On 2 December the battery returned to war, reoccupying its former positions at Le Touret. They had been given a new zone of fire, supporting the Manchesters and later the Leicesters. Claud made daily visits to the trenches, agreeing nicknames with the battalion commanders to identify prominent features and using a single gun to register the line and range to likely targets. This registration had to be carried out with great precision, as some of the chosen targets were only 100 yards from the forward trenches. The walk to and from the battery position was a hairy business. On several occasions the party came under accurate sniper fire and narrowly missed being hit, bullets striking the road creating sparks *not half a foot from our legs*. The weather in December continued to be appalling, pouring rain, fog, sleet, frost, followed by a thaw. On some days the visibility was so bad that further registration was impossible. On a night when it was Claud's turn to sleep in the dugout on the gun position, the roof began to leak, first drips and then a deluge. Eventually he did not attempt to lie down but wrapped himself in the oilskin his mother had sent him from home and sat huddled in the one dry corner. *I don't think I have ever spent a more miserable night in my life.* The Leicesters' trenches were in an indescribable state of filth *with*

water over my knees in places, and as I had gum boots on I suffered! **31**
Not surprisingly all the battery had colds.

On its return to Le Touret at the beginning of the month, action was taken to improve the brigade's communications. Telephone lines were laid from the brigade headquarters to the artillery group commander, the artillery brigade headquarters, and forward to the batteries, and from the batteries to their infantry battalions in the front line. A new pattern of telephone, the Don 3, was brought into service. It was a marked improvement on the earlier Don 1. On 10 December all the batteries received their first allocation of high explosive shells.

With Christmas approaching, Claud asked his mother if she and her friends and members of the family would make up parcels of small presents to be sent to the eight gunners who worked closely with him in his battery headquarters: the BSM, trumpeter and second trumpeter, servant, groom, pay sergeant, clerk and signals NCO. He enclosed a list of appropriate presents: socks, mittens, neck comforters, thick vests and pants, handkerchiefs, illustrated papers or a book, a packet of Navy Cut tobacco, cigarettes (the cheap ones sold in packets of five for 2d); an inexpensive pipe, safety matches, tinder cigarette lighter, chocolate or sweets, tin of cocoa or a packet of tea, Kitchener writing pad [19] and pencil, gloves and a shirt. For himself he asked for Three Nuns tobacco. And whilst she was at it, *a plum pudding for the officers and two for the sergeants would be much appreciated (with the lucky 6d inside).* Mrs Potter and her friends turned up trumps. By Christmas Eve he was asking her not to send any more mittens, scarves, balaclava helmets, gloves or pipes. All the men now had an ample supply. Queen Mary, on behalf of herself and the women of the Empire, had sent every man a woollen cholera belt *a perfectly useless thing but awfully nice of her all the same.* Princess Mary's gift was more practical, a strong pocket-sized tin containing a packet of cigarettes and another of tobacco, with a card and a small photograph of herself inside the tin. Many, like Claud, kept them for years afterwards as souvenirs.

---

[19] These Kitchener pads were smaller than the modern A5 size, coarse, lined paper that could be used on both sides. Claud wrote almost all his letters on these pads, using an indelible pencil.

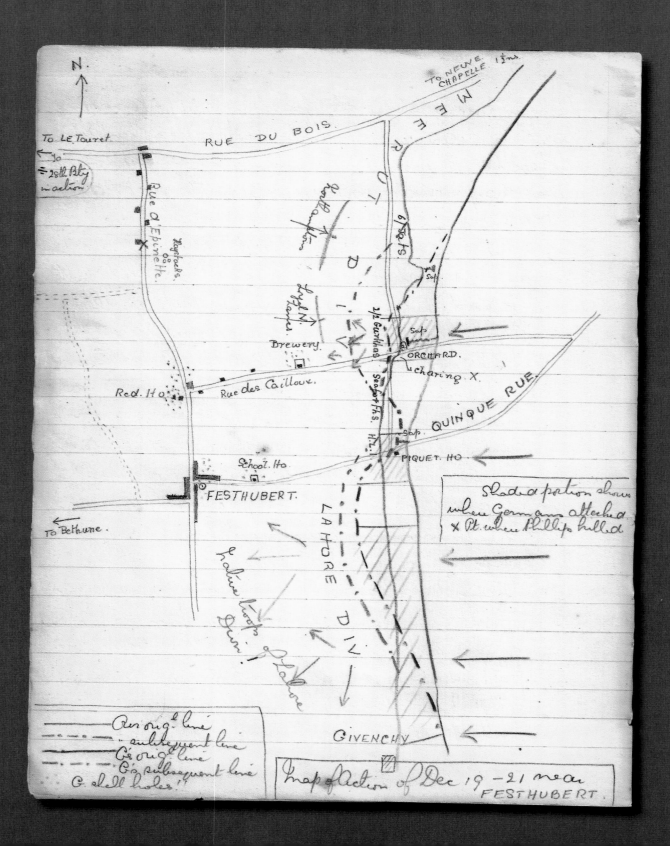

N

TO LE TOURET

RUE DU BOIS.

TO NEUVE CHAPELLE 1½ms.

To
28th Bty in action

Rue d'Epinette.

Haystacks 00

X

Loft N

Left Banks

Brewery

D I V

6 Pts.

Sap.

2/2 Gurkhas

Sap.

ORCHARD.

Charing X.

Seaforths. H.L.

Red. Ho.

Rue des Cailloux.

QUINQUE RUE.

Sap.

PIQUET. HO.

School Ho.

FESTHUBERT.

To Bethune.

Native troops of Lahore.

L A H O R E   D I V.

Shaded portion shows where Germans attacked X Pt. where Phillips killed

GIVENCHY

As orig¹ line
" subsequent line
G's orig¹ line
G's subsequent line
O shell holes!!

Map of Action of Dec 19-21 near FESTHUBERT.

The puddings arrived just in time for Christmas Day and were 33
heated up in the ubiquitous camp kettles, which were not kettles at
all but large, lidded cooking pots used for brewing up tea and stew,
and Christmas puddings. They remained an essential part of cooking
in the field for the next 40 years.

In mid December the Indian Corps was directed to mount limited
attacks on both divisional fronts to draw attention away from the I
and II Corps' offensive that was to be mounted from the area of
Messines. The Lahore Division at the southern end of the British
sector was to attack on a 300 yard front west of Givenchy.
The Meerut Division was to mount an attack to capture the trenches
in the area of the orchard on La Quinque Rue (see map facing) with
zero hour at 3.45 am on 20 December. 28 Battery's role was to support
the Leicesters. The battalion achieved complete surprise, capturing
300 yards of the enemy trench with very little loss. Unfortunately the
flank battalions failed to support them, with the result that they
were enfiladed, coming under direct machine gun fire, and were
forced to retire to their own trenches.

All that afternoon Claud's battery engaged German troops coming
up from the rear. It was assumed that they were reinforcements for a
counter attack. In fact, the Germans had already been planning to
mount a major offensive against the Indian Corps. It was pure
chance that it was arranged for the day following the Indian raids.
That night the weather was particularly bad, pouring rain driven on
a high wind and bitterly cold. The sepoys were soaked through, and
in many cases their rifles were unusable, being clogged with mud.
At dawn the Germans attacked all along the corps' front. At 9.50 am
the battery observation officer reported back to the brigade
headquarters that mines "had been sprung" all along the ridge from
Festhubert towards Givenchy, followed by the enemy quitting their
trenches and rushing into the attack with hand grenades. Twenty
minutes later he reported that the Indian trenches on the Festhubert
road had been overrun. Half an hour later the trenches held by the
Highland Light Infantry and 2/2 Gurkhas had been captured. Ten
mines were detonated in two waves along the corps' front. It was the
first time so far in the war that mines had been used. The effects were
devastating. *Earth, revetting materials, bodies and bits of equipment
flew twenty feet into the air. Everyone in the vicinity of an exploding*

mine was killed outright, whilst anyone within 50 yards was knocked senseless, dazed or otherwise rendered incapable of action.[20]

All along the front the battalions were gradually being forced back. The Germans, as well as being fresh and numerically stronger, had a plentiful supply of far more sophisticated grenades than the Indians' jam tin version.[21] The Ghurkhas, their rifles caked with mud, set them aside and unsheathed their kukris. Corrigan claims that the battalions were given little artillery support. To a certain extent Claud's entry for 20 December corroborates this. Though the improved telephone handset had been brought into use a fortnight earlier and lines laid between infantry and artillery brigade headquarters, and between the infantry in the trenches and their supporting batteries, the firing of the mines and shell fire had disrupted this well planned system of communications. Nevertheless, the commander of the Dehra Dun Brigade, which had borne the brunt of the attack on the Meerut Division's front, was to thank the batteries of 9th Brigade for their excellent shooting and always prompt cooperation.

Claud appears to have observed the battle from Red House. *When the attack began I had Burkenshaw in the OS and Robinson in the trenches. We were able to turn one section* [two guns] *on the left attack and two sections* [four guns] *on our right. We must have done a lot of damage but for about half an hour we were the only guns to fire. What on earth were the others doing, especially the battery supporting the HLI in the Lahore Division? I went to the OS towards mid-day but saw very little to fire at in the way of targets. German artillery very active though and we had a hot afternoon of it. About 20 small HE fell within a radius of 30 yards of our*

Special Order by Commander 9th Brigade RFA Christmas Day 1914

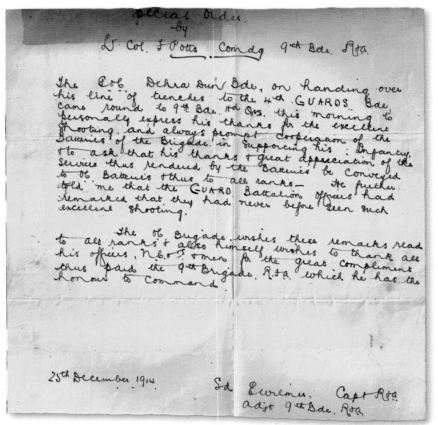

house [probably Red House], *some much closer. One hit the house behind (Glad we got the funk pit dug!). This evening the situation decidedly serious on both sides of the Seaforths, a big wedge pushed in. Though reserves all brought up, a counterattack never came off. If one can believe rumours all is not well with some of the Regiments who do not come from England. Sooner they are all packed off to their native sun, the better. A perfectly filthy day, cold and pouring rain. How I do pity the poor fellows in the trenches. Those of the Seaforths knee-deep in black, slimy mud, in the communication trenches up to their middles. Nonetheless they don't seem the slightest downhearted. In another trench two Gurkhas were drowned.*

The next day was equally filthy. *All morning no news available as to what really has happened and, though one never likes to be downhearted, things certainly did look a bit black. About 2 pm we got news that large reinforcements were being pushed up from Bethune in motor buses. They arrived at dusk and a counterattack arranged for 6 pm. We let 'em have it from every gun for half an hour but nothing happened and it appears counterattack eventually took place later with no artillery support. What a bandabast!* [22]

Claud's diary continues: *Spent most of the day in the observation station and again heavily shelled at intervals of every half hour. None actually hit the house but several only a few yards short and bits of shell, earth, etc, blown up against the front. Contrary to expectation, no heavy firing after dark and we were allowed a night's peace. During 24 hours brigade fired 2,056 rounds!*

Next day, 22 December, Claud recorded: *Had a really hot time of it today. Observation station very heavily shelled all day by all kinds of*

---

[20] Corrigan, ibid p.117.

[21] The Indian Corps version consisted of a charge of gun cotton in a tin with a fuse attached. To light the fuse, it had first to be cut to expose the core, after which the match head had to be held to the core and ignited by a matchbox, provided the box was not soaked. Corrigan, ibid p.115.

[22] 'Bandabast' is Urdu for 'arrangement'. The entry in the brigade war diary for 21 December states: "Counter-attack to start at 5.15 pm. Start delayed to 7.5 pm. Information of delay not passed to Brigade Commander until too late. At 8.5 pm he was told by 2 Brigade that the attack was proceeding and asking for assistance in best possible manner. Very large amount of ammunition expended".

36

shell. Several hit house. In afternoon simply had to shift and had a very warm time from shells and bullets whilst we were looking for another OS. Found a nice place in a loft and was up there with Sgt Maj looking around and congratulating myself on my luck when a big shrapnel burst only a few feet above me, bringing down a lot of the roof [and incidentally CFP who reached ground level in about two steps!]. Several followed and we should undoubtedly have been hit but for a stout wall that happened to be handy. Of course all our wires got cut, and we could do nothing for a long time. Eventually communications re-established about 4.15 and we then did ten minutes real good shooting at the Picquet House, observing from Sussex trenches. Things looking up today. The whole of I Corps [23] [Sir Douglas Haig] rolled up and several extra regiments of Territorials. An enormous force now in these parts. On arrival of new troops things began to be put in order a bit. New line dug behind our centre section and the right and left joined up. The Germans in the Orchard very heavily shelled, apparently with great effect as our new line was dug during the night without any interference. Apparently in yesterday's counterattack the Northamptons recovered our trenches on left of C Section all right but something went wrong with the North Lancs. About 4 companies appear to have held up their hands and surrendered without putting up anything of a fight. Poor fellows, they are nearly all immature lads of about 18 [of the original lot only about a hundred were left after Ypres] and it seems they couldn't stick the bombs, having been provided with none themselves. Why not, goodness only knows.

The marked difference between Claud's sympathetic understanding of the conduct of the young soldiers of the North Lancashires and his condemnation of the alleged failure of some of the Indian battalions, does him no credit. He made no allowance for the fact that the Indian battalions had been in the line continuously for two months, many of them suffering from trench foot. For much of that time some were still wearing the khaki drill uniforms. Only now, with winter at its height, was warm clothing being issued – serge uniforms, pullovers, gloves, great coats and flannel shirts. The Indians were expected to secure the same length of front as one of the British corps with two thirds of the manpower. There was an

---

[23] Three days later the BEF was reorganised into two Armies with Haig becoming Commander of First Army.

acute shortage of British officers. By the beginning of December, 187 were dead, wounded or missing.[24] It was becoming increasingly difficult to find as reinforcements officers who understood the Indian soldier, the patriarchal relationship between an officer and his sepoys, and who spoke their language, understood their traditions and knew their homelands.

There are many instances of individual bravery and devotion to duty in the service of the Empire, despite the fact that the soldiers were fighting in conditions of landscape and weather that none had previously experienced. Claud's remark that *all was not well* in some regiments is not borne out by history, though in time, due to the heavy casualties amongst British officers with Indian army experience, the standards of Indian units did decline.[25] However, Haig, then commanding I Corps, who visited the Indian Corps headquarters in late November, did recall that he found "an air of dejection and despondency. I came away with a feeling that things were not altogether in an efficient state".[26]

Claud's diary continues on 23 December, *Up at 6 am, to observation station at dawn. Found new place where can see quite well but we hadn't been there an hour before the German guns were on to it. They shelled all the houses along that particular road. One hit the house next door and brought down the roof, about six fell in the yard just behind ours. A brick wall is a comfort on such occasions. All very quiet today apart from the shelling. Everything has now been put straight and troops rolling up every hour. The Guards Brigade arrived today, a fine looking lot. We are now covering the Sussex who have taken over the Seaforth's trenches. Thick mist and snow all morning, later turning to rain. Hear that we are going for a rest in a few days at Lillers. The whole of the Indian Corps is being replaced by I Corps. Our wretched infantry have fairly earned a rest. They have had an awful time and exceedingly heavy casualties.* Next day Claud returned to the Red House from where he shelled Picquet House and Snipers' House at intervals. The front had gone quiet, but the Grenadiers who had taken over from the Sussex had already suffered a good many casualties.

[24] Corrigan, ibid p.225. Total figures for killed, wounded and missing were 187 officers, 95 Viceroy Commissioned Officers (VCOs) and 1,935 Indian soldiers.

[25] Corrigan, ibid p.246.

[26] Brown, p.225 quoting Robert Blake *The Private Papers of Douglas Haig 1914–1919*, p.78.

Christmas Day was seasonable, at least as far as the weather was concerned, a fine day with a hard hoar frost. *We fired twice during the night at the Guards' request and evidently did good work, stopping two German rushes completely. To OP* [the nomenclature had been changed from 'observation station' to the present day 'observation post'] *in Brewery at dawn. Nothing to be seen as very thick mist. Everything very quiet except for sniping. OC Grenadiers loud in our praise over yesterday's and last night's shooting.* The commander of the Guards Brigade, Lord Cavan, came personally to thank Claud and his battery for their excellent support. *I need scarcely say that his Lordship was very gratified at one of his near relations being able to do something for him!!!* [27] It was the day that the historic Christmas truce took place when along about half the BEF front, including at least one of the Indian Corps battalions, the British and German soldiers came out of their trenches to meet, exchange souvenirs and play football. Claud makes no mention of it. The fierce Battle of Festubert was only now drawing to a close. According to a German communiqué, which Claud described as *the truest account of all*, 19 officers and 810 men, British and native, had been taken prisoner and 14 machine guns and other war material captured. The British, it added, left over 3,000 dead on the field and an 'Englishman' asked for a cessation of hostilities to bury their dead.

On St Stephen's Day, the Indian Corps was at last relieved. 9th Brigade, including Claud's battery, was allocated a rest area at Ames, ten miles west of Bethune and four miles to the south of Lillers. The march was carried out by night in filthy weather, sleet and rain driven on a strong wind. *Arrived 8.15 pm, all very cold and thoroughly miserable, to find we had awful accommodation for officers, men and horses.* The brigade was to remain there for five weeks.

On New Year's Day Lieutenant Colonel F Potts, the artillery brigade commander, recorded in his headquarters war diary: "Again reported inadequate accommodation for men and horses. State of fields and roads extremely bad, being inches deep in mud. The whole locality is very damp and apparently unhealthy, and I fear will affect the

[27] Lord Lambert, 10th Earl of Cavan, commanded 4th Guards Brigade from 1914 to 1915, XIV Corps from 1916 to 1917 in the rank of lieutenant general, C-in-C BEF 1918 to 1919, and ended up as Chief of the Imperial General Staff from 1922 to 1926. How he was a 'near relation' I have not been able to discover.

efficiency of the brigade." In mid November Potts had recorded that, considering the extreme range of temperature to which they had been subjected, the horses brought from India had kept in remarkably good condition. A certain number had lately shown slight temperatures, no doubt partly due to the irregular issue of forage. The same forage was rarely issued on two consecutive days, one day all oats, the next all grain, the next grain and barley, then back to oats again. The barley on some occasions had to be rejected, having been loaded during the rain in Bombay. Now at Ames, Potts was becoming very anxious about the horses' health, for without them the brigade would be unable to move. He recorded that many were suffering from 'greasy heels', an equine form of trench feet, through standing all day in the open in the mud. It was said to be infectious, but the vets could not treat the outbreaks as long as the horses were out in the open. Daily there was a shortage of hay at the refuelling point and, the local farms being poor, hay was difficult to obtain locally in sufficient quantities. Eventually, after Potts had made repeated complaints to the staff, two of the batteries were moved to nearby villages, leaving Claud's battery in Ames. By the middle of the month all the horses were under cover. It is estimated that eight million horses died during the war, most from exposure, disease and starvation. Often they were so hungry that they ate their sodden rugs and choked to death on the buckles.[28]

There was a sense of relief when news came through during a snow storm at the end of the month that the brigade was to return to the firing line. They were all heartily sick of Ames. In five weeks there had been only three days without rain. Claud said he had never seen mud like it and wondered if there was any truth in the theory that prolonged bombardment caused the rain. Despite the conditions the staff had insisted on drill order parades and twice a week an eight mile route march on foot. There was a church service held in a local girls' school to mark a day of intercession for the success of the Allies, by command of the King. On another occasion the Indian Corps commander inspected a dismounted parade of the brigade, formed up in an orchard. A draft of 20 reinforcements arrived from the base depot at Havre. Courses were held on the new Don 3 telephone and

---

[28] *Animals in War*, Jilly Cooper, quoted in *The Daily Telegraph* article of November 2004, describing the unveiling of the Animals in War Memorial in Park Lane by the Princess Royal.

demonstrations given to all officers and senior ranks on the new Mills hand grenade, which in the conditions of trench warfare had assumed a new importance. Everyone had baths at Lillers, where they were issued with a complete change of underclothing.

From all this Claud managed to escape for a week. By now a system of home leave had been introduced, officers and soldiers being selected on a roster basis, though there were many complaints that officers were granted leave more often than their men. He wrote to warn his mother of his arrival, following it up with a telegram from Folkestone. *I may get a lift in a motor car to Boulogne, in which case I shall catch the 2.30 pm boat at Boulogne and arrive in London (Victoria) some time on Wednesday evening, getting home in time for dinner.*

It must have been very hard to adjust to the contrast between, on the one hand the fierce fighting of December, the high explosives, the constant danger, the lack of sleep and in January the mud and rain of Ames, and on the other the comfort of his mother's home in an English suburb hardly touched by war, regular meals and baths, uninterrupted sleep in a warm, comfortable, dry bed and the gentle company of women. Even the weather was fine. There is no mention of how he spent his leave, beyond a reminder that he had promised to take his mother to see 'David Copperfield' *months before we had even thought about any war.* Nor is there any mention in any of his letters or diary of a particular woman friend. He was an attractive man, gentle, with an old world courtesy, brought up in a loving family in the last 20 years of the Victorian era. Perhaps the years in India had given him little opportunity to form an attachment; single women sent out East to find a husband were unkindly referred to as the 'fishing fleet'. Perhaps like many solders he felt it would be wrong to become too involved with a woman when the chances of living through the war were so slim.

It must have been very hard to return to the front, yet for many it was a relief. As a gunner subaltern wrote in 1917: "I feel that I really belong at the front. Even when I got back to England on leave, it seemed to me that I belonged at the front, that the leave was only an interlude. In a way I was quite ready to get back. That was reinforced by the fact that my family didn't understand what was happening out there, and I didn't really want them to know about it. So when I was talking to my parents or my sisters, I had to pretend it was all very nice out there, and I had to describe a world that wasn't real at all. The real world was the one that I had to get back to, and I felt no compunction about getting away when the leave was over." [29]

His leave over, Claud caught an early train from Bromley to Victoria during the morning rush hour. *En route a lot of vulgar fellows with their 'Daily Chronicles'* came into the carriage. Like a scene from *The Railway Children*, neighbours came to the bottom of their garden to wave as the boat train went by. That evening the lorry dropped him off at Ames, but at the wrong corner, leaving him to walk a mile to his billet with his luggage. It was still raining when he returned to the Le Touret gun position on 1 February via the rest area at Ames, followed four days later by the brigade. He found a change had taken place in the topography of the battlefield. Due to the incessant rain the trenches were no longer habitable. Both sides had resorted to building sandbagged redoubts, weakly held about 20 yards apart and connected to each other by shallow trenches. Guns were no longer dug in but deployed above ground protected by sandbag walls. 'No Man's Land' had become a marsh and, apart from shelling and snipers, there was little activity on either side. "Ghastly conditions such as these, which made simple existence difficult for both sides, encouraged a certain live-and-let-live attitude." [30]

A new OP had been established opposite the Brewery. The previous one in Red House was now so dilapidated that it looked as if one more explosion would collapse it completely. The old grey cat and the black kitten were still in residence, looking fat and sleek, and were probably the reason that the other residents, the pigeons, had all disappeared.

During the next ten days that the brigade artillery brigade spent in the line, the sector was very quiet. From the new OP Claud could see into lengths of the German trenches and watched them

---

[29] From Max Aitkin, *Voices of The Great War, Sunday Times* and Imperial War Museum quoted in the programme for *Journey's End* by R C Sherriff, Duke of York's Theatre, London, Winter, 2004.

[30] Holmes, ibid p.247.

42

smoking and making their meals. It was apparent that they were not contemplating making an attack. There was nothing going on. It was too cold to read or write, so the OP party kept warm by walking up and down the loft sucking Mrs Potter's latest resupply of Bulls Eyes. On 13 January the battery was relieved and rode back to St Floris, 11 miles to the north west on the Lys canal, another miserable billet with precious little cover for man or beast. Pouring rain and a strong, bitterly cold wind. *Everyone is pretty fed up. The mud is too disgusting for words. With our horses standing fetlock deep in black slime it is well nigh impossible to get them groomed.* However, once again Claud escaped. Three days later he received orders to report to the War Office. It was the summons he had foreseen and dreaded, a staff appointment in Kitchener's New Army. He wished then that he had never attended the Staff College course at Quetta, but the posting was inevitable. In the first five months of the war 56 staff officers with the BEF had been killed.[31] After nine months about half the Staff College graduates were dead or wounded "… often falling gallantly at places where they should not have been…" having volunteered to return to their units (and forfeited their staff pay) as soon as war was declared. [32]

Claud said goodbye to his battery next day with great regret. *I have spent a very happy time with 28 Battery,* he wrote. *I think we had a very good show and all pulled along very well together.* He obtained a lift in the battery mess cart to Hazebrouck and thence by train to Boulogne. The regular ferry had been cancelled due to U-boat activity in the Channel, but he obtained a passage on a cargo boat out of Dieppe that had been landing a cargo of 15 inch guns and ammunition. [33] After an exceedingly rough crossing, he reported to the War Office and was told to go home and await orders. He telegraphed his mother from Victoria: *Just arrived home on posting to staff, should be back about lunch.*

---

[31] *The Old Contemptibles,* ibid p.106.

[32] Holmes, ibid p.225.

[33] Probably the obsolete BLC 15 pounder gun issued to the Territorial units

**Chapter 4 THE BATTLE OF LOOS
26 September 1915**

Loos was to be the largest battle ever fought by the British army up to that time, and for the first time untried divisions of the New Army were to play a major role. The task of providing a reserve to exploit initial success was allocated to XI Corps, consisting of the newly formed Guards Division under command of Lord Cavan and 21st and 24th Divisions. In March, a month after his return from France, Claud had received orders to report to Shoreham in Sussex to take over the post of Deputy Assistant Adjutant and Quartermaster General (DAA & QMG) of 24th Division.

Claud did not keep up his diary during the raising and training of the division, but a reference to him occurs in the letters of a 22 year old American, Harry Butters. The son of wealthy parents from California, Butters came to England in February 1915 to enlist in the British army. Initially he was granted a commission in the Royal Warwicks, but, on hearing a talk by Claud on his experiences commanding a field battery in France, Butters was determined to transfer to the artillery. "Major Potter seemed to be quite a charming fellow and quite approachable, so after the lecture I bolted up and collared him before he had a chance to break away – asked him if he could spare me some of his time in the next two or three days, and was told to come to the divisional headquarters at any time during work hours." Butters was a determined young man. He called on Claud the next day. Though he must have been very busy on more pressing matters involved in the raising of a division, Claud arranged

44

for Butters to meet the divisional commander and then smoothed the way to ensure that he was attached to an artillery brigade, initially in the divisional ammunition column, but later, under pressure from the ever persistent Butters, to command a section of guns in a field battery. "I was incoherent in thanking him, for I had been under rotten suspense. I only remembered telling him I was more grateful to him than any one I had ever met in my life, and that I was going to thank him by making myself the best officer he had ever arranged a transfer for. I hope some day I shall serve under him." Possibly Claud saw in him a man more confident and mature than the subalterns being commissioned straight from their Officer Training Corps, a young man who would serve the Royal Artillery well. They met once more, in France as 24th Division was forming up for the advance to Loos. "He is a dear," Butters wrote to his brother and sister in California. "You must both meet him when you come over to witness the triumphal return of our armies in 191-?" Sadly, it was not to be. In August 1916 he was hit by a gas shell and killed instantly. He is buried in the war cemetery at Meaulte, a mile south of Albert. [34]

One of the enduring images of the Great War is the poster of Lord Kitchener, the Secretary of State for War, finger pointing and the injunction 'Your Country Needs You'. It is said that from whatever angle you look at the poster the eyes seem to be staring and the index finger pointing at you. Long queues formed outside recruiting centres across the country as hundreds of thousands of men volunteered to enlist. On one day alone over 33,000 enlisted. In fewer than three months there was sufficient manpower to create five new armies, the foundations for 30 divisions. No plans had been made in advance to cope with this huge expansion. There was a shortage of everything: accommodation, uniforms, weapons, ammunition, training areas, draught horses, harnesses and vehicles.

Because of a shortage of khaki cloth, most of the new recruits had to wear blue uniforms, with forage caps and civilian overcoats. Arms drill was carried out using broomsticks. Accommodation was Spartan, mainly in six men bell tents. Feeding was poor. Above all there was a chronic shortage of experienced officers and NCOs.

[34] *Harry Butters RFA 'An American Citizen'. Life and War Letters*, edited by Mrs Denis O'Sullivan. Reprinted from the original by Lightning Source UK Ltd, September 2010.

Some boys still at public schools were granted immediate commissions on the strength of their membership of their schools' Officer Training Corps. One artillery brigade was formed round a retired colonel and four new second lieutenants.[35] At the time of Loos in the 21st and 24th Divisions, only one of the divisional commanders, two of the eight brigade commanders and one of the 26 battalion commanders were serving in the regular army. Just 30 of the regimental officers had regular army experience, the rest being wartime volunteers with no more than a year's service, and with all but a few weeks of that in England.[36]

When the raising and training of 24th Division was complete, Claud returned to keeping his dairy, opening a new volume on 22 August 1915. He had been detailed as a member of the divisional advance party for the move across the Channel. In the early hours of the morning they drove from Aldershot to Southampton. Despite dusty roads, especially around Winchester, they made good time, completing the 57 mile journey in under two hours, and embarked on the transport *Mona's Queen*, one of the Isle of Man paddle steamers. The boat was crowded with 1,500 men on board, mainly the members of a labour battalion *navvies in uniform, the most awful lot of hooligans you ever saw.* The stench of humanity was overpowering and there was no room to move about. Fortunately the crossing, with an escort of two destroyers, was smooth. They disembarked at Le Havre the following morning and were put up in the Hotel de Normandie, *apartments et chambres avec salle de bains particulière.* They were charged FF20 a day and, as the accommodation allowance was only FF6, they were FF14 a day out of pocket. There was little he could do over the next few days, other than check on the accommodation for the main body in camps around the port and acquaint himself with the layout of the docks and routes to railway stations.

Claud fretted that he would have been employed more profitably if he had remained in England with divisional headquarters. With time on their hands three of the party took a steamer across the mouth of the estuary of the Seine to the resort town of Trouville. The place was deserted except for a large number of children and a few of the

---

[35] Farndale, ibid p.86.

[36] Holmes, ibid p.176.

demi-mondaines who were accustomed to coming down from Paris for the summer season, parading around in the most lovely bathing costumes, but seldom venturing into the water. The day was hot. The three officers spent the time walking on the sands and helping the children dig for lampreys, a species of eel. Whilst waiting in Le Havre, Claud spent an evening at a concert in the opera house, given by one of Miss Lena Ashwell's concert parties, which he enjoyed.[37] His time at Le Havre was a gentle prelude, the last hours of sanity before the blood bath that was to follow four weeks later.

By 2 September the last transports had arrived and the division had moved into a concentration area in the neighbourhood of Montreuil [38] in the rich agricultural district of Artois, a land of rolling hills and deep valleys, *so peaceful and pretty*. The area was, however, sparsely populated so that farms and barns were far apart, and as a result the divisions were widely dispersed. Claud followed on by motor, given a lift by a Colonel Horsbrough, a journey of 150 miles. He found the divisional headquarters at Royon, billeted in a *château* belonging to the Baron de Haute-au-Cloque. The main rooms, taken over as an officers' mess and offices, were palatial, the furniture Louis XIV. The sleeping quarters were cramped. Claud shared a small room with a fellow officer, but later the Baron moved him into his best bedroom. Claud became very friendly with the family, including the four year old daughter and Mademoiselle, the niece. He was invited to tea and games of bridge, and walked in the gardens with the Baroness. His schoolboy French was improving fast. *Magnificent day,* he wrote on 8 September. *Not much doing. Gunfire very distinct, wind being in east. Tea with the Baroness and Mademoiselle (Seth-Smith as chaperone!). Camp fire and concert after dinner. Bed 11 pm.*

[37] Lena Ashwell began her early acting career in a modest way, understudying the great Ellen Terry, whose actor brother was a friend of Claud's parents. By 1906 Miss Ashwell was one of the most famous and best loved actresses in England. When the war broke out, she formed a number of concert parties to entertain the troops in France and the Middle East. By the end of the war there were 25 of them, made up of established singers, instrumentalists and entertainers. On occasions they performed excerpts from Shakespeare's plays. She was awarded an OBE, married Sir Henry Simpson, the Royal obstetrician, who was a surgeon at Queen Elizabeth's birth. She died in 1956, aged 83. Extracted from *The Golden Age of British Theatre (1880–1920)* by Sydney Higgins.

[38] Montreuil is a mediaeval town with a castle within a citadel, majestic walls and ramparts. It was the scene for an episode in Victor Hugo's *Les Miserables*. Agincourt is nine miles to the east. In 1916 Montreuil became the location for Haig's GHQ.

Meanwhile the division settled in and carried out training. Small parties of officers and men were sent forward to obtain experience of the front. Claud was very busy, particularly trying to devise a system of casualty reporting that would work smoothly despite the inexperience and poor quality of his clerical staff. He paid two visits to St Omer, to the north of Montreuil [39] where XI Corps Commander, Lieutenant General Sir Richard Hacking, had set up his headquarters. He attended a lecture on gas and tested the effectiveness of his helmet by walking through a gas filled trench. He visited the divisional artillery, the batteries already being deployed in support of First Army south of La Bassée canal five miles from Le Touret, his old battery position in December 1914. He was encouraged by all he saw. He told his mother: *Everybody out here is most awfully optimistic about the war. They are all the same and feel absolutely confident that it is only a matter of time now. The men are in fine condition too. I never felt prouder of the army or felt more confident of our ultimate success.* They were not to know that Haig, the First Army commander, had grave misgivings about the forthcoming battle.

During that summer General Joffre, Chief of the French General Staff, had been exerting pressure on the Allies to mount a new offensive on the Western front with the British attacking in the north in the coal mining district between La Bassée canal and Lens, whilst the French would attack in two widely separated areas, Arras-Lens and Rheims. A successful breakthrough was to be a signal for a general offensive along the whole front, pushing the Germans back behind the Meuse and possibly ending the war.

Kitchener, the Secretary of State for War, and Sir John French, Commander-in-Chief of the British Expeditionary Force, gave their lukewarm support, but Haig believed that an attack in the Lens sector at the present time would be a grave error. He had seen the ground for himself, an area of "huge black slag heaps, little, sordid dirty villages and its roads made of black mud a foot deep."[40]

---

[39] In a letter from Le Havre Claud had told his mother to pay particular notice to postscripts in future letters. Now he added a nonsensical PS in which the first letter of each word spelt out 'Montreuil'. Another PS in a later letter told her that corps headquarters was at St Omer. Thereafter he seems to have decided that this method of getting round the censor was not in order.

[40] *The Imperial War Museum Book of the Western Front*, ibid p.83.

48

Whilst the relatively high ground in the south afforded good observation for the British, the flat land in the north was overlooked by the German defences. After the Battle of Neuve Chapelle in March 1915, the Germans had learnt the lesson of defence in depth, with two lines 4,000 yards apart, a distance chosen deliberately as it would force the opposing artillery to redeploy during the battle to bring the second line within its range. They had set out their defences at Lens on this basis, with their second line three miles behind the first. Every village had been turned into a fortress, miners' cottages into machine gun nests, whilst the great pithead pylons provided observation stations with a wide view over much of the battlefield. Haig was all too well aware that he was faced with an acute shortage of artillery, particularly heavy guns and shells. German armament factories were producing 250,000 rounds a day, the British 22,000. However, he was persuaded that the shortage of artillery support might be offset by the use of gas. The German gas masks gave protection for 30 minutes. If the gas cloud could be made to linger for 40 minutes, it would compensate for the limited artillery support.[41] The attack was to be mounted by I Corps in the north, consisting of 2nd, 7th and 9th Divisions and IV Corps in the south with 1st, 15th and 47th Divisions. XI Corps, consisting of the Cavalry Division, the newly formed Guards Division and the so far unblooded 21st and 24th Divisions, would provide the general reserve.

On the night of 21 September, as the preliminary barrage began, 24th Division set out on its march to the front, arriving after midnight in an area 20 miles east of Montreuil. Claud had gone on ahead to arrange billets for the divisional headquarters at Bomy. It was an early example of their inexperience that the units, instead of providing mounted billeting parties, had sent them ahead on foot, with the result that they had no time to allocate billets before their people arrived. Some lost their way and would not have arrived at all if Claud had not gone out in a motor car in the middle of the night and guided them in. Luckily it was a mild, dry night. It was 3.30 am by the time he got to bed.

They moved on next night, another 16 miles to the east to an area just north of Lillers. Some of the units arrived very tired, with many

[41] This was the first use of gas by the Allies. The Germans had used it with considerable success at the Second Battle of Ypres in April and May when, but for the gallantry of the Canadian division and a makeshift British force, they would have captured the town.

stragglers. Divisional headquarters was at Busnes in a *château* that had been used as a billet since the early days of the war, a place so filthy and smelly that Claud slept out in the garden, not that he got much sleep. It was 2.30 am before he got to bed after a busy day.

Next day Claud went forward to reconnoitre routes into the reserves area south east of Bethune. On 24 September orders were received for the division to move to the Bethune-Beuvry area that night. It arrived in the early hours of the morning, a short march, but the rain was pouring down and the roads were in an awful state. Again advance parties had failed to make arrangements for their units, which arrived to find no billets, camps or guides, and they made little effort to help themselves. *They will learn by degrees with the help of bitter experience*, Claud noted.

Before leaving Busnes the divisional headquarters had been visited by Second Lieutenant Wales, who was to become King Edward VIII. He had brought some much needed machine gun parts. *He's only about five feet high but very smart and soldierly in appearance and, I hear, exceedingly popular with all.*

On 25 September Claud and the divisional staff were up early, anxiously waiting for news of the great attack. Everything depended on the wind. If that was unfavourable, the chlorine gas could not be used and an alternative plan would have to be followed, a much less ambitious assault on a two division front. It very nearly was. The day dawned calm, almost windless, but with a slight breeze blowing at 5.15 am Haig decided to order the gas to be released. It was spasmodically successful, drifting into the enemy trenches on the right but too slow and slight for full effect. On the left it drifted back into the British line, but caused only seven fatalities. The assault was launched at 6.30 am, an hour after the gas attack. On the right it went well with the Jocks of 15th Division nearly achieving a breakthrough, whilst 7th and 9th Divisions at the centre made good progress. The moment had come to commit the reserve corps. It was then that the battle was lost.

Despite Haig's objections, French had insisted on keeping the reserve divisions under his control, well back, 16 miles to the north west, and refused to release them until he had been up to the front to see the situation for himself. Vital time was lost. The divisions did not receive orders to move forward to a preliminary position behind Vermelles until 9 am. Claud and a fellow staff officer pushed on ahead to find a report centre, selecting the cellar of a shell shattered house in the town. Haig, believing that the forward divisions were about to achieve a breakthrough, had called forward one of the cavalry divisions to exploit the success.[42] The main Bethune-Vermelles road, the only road forward, was packed with troops and transport, and thousands of cavalry moving up, whilst hundreds of wounded and German prisoners moved in the opposite direction. Vermelles was *a seething mass of disorganised traffic rapidly getting out of control* as the town came under heavy shellfire. Hampered by the traffic chaos, the length of the march and the pouring rain, the divisions did not arrive until late in the afternoon, too late to mount an attack that day. Claud spent the night rounding up the divisional first line transport which had been harboured in a very exposed area, forward of Vermelles and moving them back behind the town. He did not get to bed all night.

The following morning, 26 September, the two New Army divisions moved into position and at 11 am mounted their attack against the German second line. It was too late. By then the enemy had regained some lost ground in counter attacks and during the night had reinforced the front with men, more machine guns and wire. According to Claud's account, 24th Division was supposed to be supported by 1st Division on their left, but they sent forward only one battalion, which was soon knocked out, whilst their fellow New Army division, 21st Division, on their right never moved forward at all, leaving the 24th Division exposed on both flanks. They reached the wire but it was uncut. They were coming under intense enfilade fire and shells from their own artillery were falling amongst them. They had no choice but to retire, *carried out in a most creditable manner with no running away.*

John Keegan quotes a graphic description of the scene: "They moved forward in ten columns, each about a thousand men, all advancing as if carrying out a parade ground drill. The German defenders were

---

[42] The last veteran of the Cavalry Corps to be present at the battle, Albert 'Smiler' Marshall, of the Essex Yeomanry, died in May 2005, aged 108.

astounded by the sight of an entire front covered with the enemy's infantry. They stood up, some even on the parapet of the trench, and fired triumphantly into the mass of men advancing across the open grassland. The machine gunners had opened fire at 1,500 yards range. Never had machine guns such straightforward work to do. With barrels becoming hot and swimming in oil, they traversed to and fro along the enemy's ranks. One machine gun alone fired 12,500 rounds that afternoon. The effect was devastating. The enemy could be seen falling literally in hundreds but they continued their march in good order and without interruption until they reached the unbroken wire of the Germans' second position. Confronted by this impenetrable obstacle, the survivors turned and began to retire. The German machine gunners, nauseated by the spectacle of the corpse field of Loos, held their fire, as the British turned and retreated, so great was their feeling of compassion and mercy after such a victory. The 12 attacking battalions, some 10,000 strong, lost 8,000 officers and men in under four hours." [43]

Somehow Claud found time to write up his diary for what he described *as a dreadful day*. For the first time he criticised the higher command. *No doubt whole attack had failed, due in my private opinion to the same old thing, vis <u>bad management</u> on the part of those above.* He recorded over four pages the reasons for the failure as he saw them, summing up with the bitter comment: *It seems inconceivable that two divisions who had absolutely no experience whatsoever of the present day trench warfare should be pushed up to make an attack on a grand scale over ground they had never seen and knew nothing about, without any definite information about anything and no plan for artillery support.*

As the battle raged, traffic conditions on the only road to the front, through Vermelles, had deteriorated further, with three or four lines of traffic, artillery and ammunition resupply columns trying to get forward and ambulances bringing the wounded back. Shells were dropping into the town. Some hit the divisional headquarters, one bursting very close to Claud, killing a man a few

---

[43] F. Forstner, *Das Reserve Infanterie Regiment 15*, Berlin, 1929, quoted in John Keegan *The First World War*, p.218.

yards off and wounding two officers and three horses. It was fortunate that the straffing was not heavier, otherwise casualties would have been enormous. The cooks could not get up for hours and when they did they had lost all touch with their units, who got no food as a consequence. Claud managed to get 100,000 rations from Bethune and collected 300 petrol tins which he filled up with water and sent forward by lorry. He spent a second night without sleep.

The following day, 27 September, the Guards Division took over the line allowing the two New Army divisions to be withdrawn. They were spent. They could do no more. *I can't altogether blame them*, Claud wrote. *It was the first time they had been in a fight, had no experience whatsoever of trench warfare, were lacking in bombs, got no food or water, all staff gone, in fact everything was against them.*

For the next two days the division was bivouacked in open fields behind Vermelles on either side of the Lens-Bethune road. Luckily it was fine and the staff ensured that everyone was provided with a hot meal. Again Claud got practically no sleep and was beginning to feel exhausted. He spent all day trying to replace lost equipment and collecting casualty reports. The division had lost 186 officers and 4,400 men out of 20,000. Eight commanding officers were dead. One battalion had lost 23 and another 24 of their 29 officers. By the end of the battle three of the nine divisional commanders and one brigade commander had been killed and two brigade commanders wounded.

On the 29 September the division moved back to a quiet area just north of Lillers, the infantry by train, the mounted troops on the road. Claud and the staff captain went ahead and did a rapid allocation of billets as the trains had already begun to arrive. He snatched an hour's sleep on the floor of a café in Berguette. In his first letter to his mother in sixteen days, he told her, *In five days I got two hours total sleep. I thought at one time I should never stick it and felt like breaking down with the strain. After the big fight everything was in a hopeless state of disorganisation, and I had a pretty stiff job getting things straight.*

Liddell Hart summed up the disastrous battle: "Never surely were novice divisions thrown into a vital stroke in a more difficult or absurd manner and in an atmosphere of greater misconception of the situation in all quarters. This amply explains their subsequent failure when their belated attack was at last launched at 11 am on the 26th and redresses the hasty judgements which were spread at the time – a stigma that was slow to fade. That in courage they were not lacking is clear and equally that its fruits were reduced by their rawness, by that of their staff still more."[44]

21st Division had suffered such heavy casualties that it was out of action until the Somme battle in 1916. By the end of the war it had sustained 55,581 casualties.[45]

---

[44] Liddell Hart, ibid p.265.

[45] Holmes, ibid pp. 274-275.

Chapter 5   **YPRES SALIENT**
                 October 1915 – July 1916

In the aftermath of the disaster at Loos, it was apparent that the inexperienced New Army divisions must be bolstered by replacing one brigade in each division with a seasoned brigade from the regular army. In 24th Division, 71st Brigade was replaced by 17th Brigade of 6th Division in mid October. Major General J E Capper took command of the division.[46] To Claud's intense relief the AA & QMG who, he told his mother, *went*

---

[46] Sir John Edward Capper, whose brother Tommy had been one of the three divisional commanders killed at Loos, was the pioneer of army aviation. In the first decade of the century he worked closely with Sam Cody, developing the first military airship. Cody, a colourful character, had been a cowboy in the 'Wild West' where he had ridden the same cattle trails as Buffalo Bill, played the same roulette tables as Wyatt Earp and competed with Annie Oakley in sharp-shooting. He came to England with a theatrical show depicting life in the 'West'. When this failed, he turned to kites, including models large enough to lift a man. These were so successful that the army engaged him as Chief Instructor in kiting at the Balloon School in Andover.

From 1905 to 1910 Capper was Commandant of the Balloon School. Following the successful airship flight, he became the first man ever to fly as a passenger in an aeroplane, piloted by Cody, on a two mile flight over Laffin's Plain at Farnborough. In 1913 he gave a lecture to the Staff College on 'The effects of aircraft in war', including their potential for tactical reconnaissance, transmission of information, offensive action and direction of artillery fire. With good reason he is regarded by many as the founder of the Royal Flying Corps.

When war began Capper was appointed Chief Engineer III Corps and Second Army. He commanded 24th Division from 1915 to 1917, followed by being appointed the Director General to the new Tank Corps. He retired in 1925 as Lieutenant Governor of Guernsey, served in the Home Guard at the age of 79 and died in 1955.

half off his rocker at Loos and had our department in such a hopeless state of confusion that it was impossible to carry on properly was replaced by a gunner, Lieutenant Colonel J F I H Doyle, brother of Sir Arthur Conan Doyle, the renowned author and creator of 'Sherlock Holmes'.

For the first fortnight in October the division settled in a rest area west of Poperinghe, with the headquarters at Steenvoorde. It was an unpleasant part of the country, churned to mud by heavy rain. Walking along the *pavé* roads, it was very hard to stand up. There was a shortage of accommodation for men and horses, as large numbers of reinforcements began to arrive to replace the casualties at Loos. *We begin to look like a division again.*

On 15 October the division took over a part of the front running from St Eloi to near Hill 60 on the south side of the salient from 17th Division. One brigade occupied the trenches, backed up by a second in reserve and the remainder of the division, including the headquarters, at Reninghelst, ten miles south east of Poperinghe. Though in later times this sector of the line and north through Sanctuary Wood to Hooge was to become one of the most fiercely contested parts of the salient, it was for the moment quiet. The weather was less severe than it had been in the previous winter.

As the division settled down, demands on the staff eased. At last Claud was getting to bed before midnight. From now on he would visit both the administrative units, which were his main responsibility, and the battalions manning the trenches, going out on these 'trench walks' several times each week, usually taking the car or riding to the rear divisional area and then continuing on foot. He walked miles. Soon he was telling his mother that he had been able to take in his belt by one hole. He was sending his boots back to Bromley to be repaired, as they were the only ones that did not chaff his chilblains. His Wellingtons had worn right through in the sole. He recorded in his diary neat sketches, showing the route he had taken in coloured pencil, and the names of old friends he had met on the way – from the Indian days, from the 'Shop', the Indian Staff College at Quetta, and school friends from Marlborough.

There were several occasions when he had narrow escapes from being killed or wounded. Indeed it seemed that he had a charmed life.

At Sanctuary Wood he was *nearly copped by a sniper who hit the parapet by my head. Rotten shooting at only 50 yards range!* [47] Near Hellfire Corner the driving band of a 5.9" howitzer shell hit him on the shoulder, but he escaped with a bruise. Four days later at Hooge on a visit to the mine crater that marked the front line, a shell fragment hit him on the other shoulder. Again he was only bruised. After this visit he wrote, *Altogether a first class day and most exciting, with glorious weather and splendid views.* [48] He seems to have thrived on the excitement, living life to the full, as if each one might be his last, as well it might have been. But there was more to it than that. It was essential that staff officers were seen in the forward areas, sharing some of the dangers and discomforts of the men in the trenches.

Battalions often regarded the staff as people who lived relatively comfortable lives out of harm's way. Their record is much maligned in the histories of the war. "Being on the staff of a fighting formation was certainly no sinecure." Holmes writes. "There were few if any who did not work a fourteen hour day and who were not to be found at work far into the night. Most general staff officers did some work before breakfast, took an hour for lunch, perhaps take a walk for their health and then work to dinner, returning to their offices afterwards. Men collapsed at their desks with the strain.... Perhaps the glacis plate of historiography is now too thick to let us get close to them.... But let us at least judge them for what they were: by and large honest, brave, hard-working... all too well aware of the consequences of their mistakes, and by no means ignorant of what they were expecting men to do or the circumstances in which they had to do it." [49]

The first of Claud's 'trench walks' was to visit a battalion of the Middlesex Regiment holding the trenches in front of St Eloi. Here the German line ran along the top of the ridge from Hooge to Wytschaete, dominating the British trenches. The opposing lines were never more than 150 yards apart. At St Eloi, where a mound of earth or a tumulus known as the 'Mound', overlooked the whole area, the gap was no more than 40 yards. Claud recorded that the front line left very much

---

[47] Staff officers were easy targets for snipers with the red bands around their hats and red and gold collar tabs. In early 1916 steel helmets were introduced.

[48] It was early February.

[49] Holmes, ibid pp. 238, 239 and 242.

to be desired, lacking back cover, and would soon be blown to bits by heavy shelling. Parts of the communication trenches were too straight and exposed to enfilade fire. For the moment, it was quiet; they hardly heard a bullet fired. He and his escort, the battalion bombing officer, had gone to St Eloi by way of Ypres. *It is indeed a wonderful sight and most awe inspiring, literally a city of the dead. It made me feel quite creepy to be there. It looks as if it has been visited by a terrible earthquake. Not a house that isn't ruined. Nothing left of the Cloth Hall, a mere shell. The magnificent cathedral tower still standing, one face only, but a few more shells will bring it down.*

John Giles in his book *The Ypres Salient* describes conditions in the shattered city. "Day after day, week after week, month after month, HE shells, including the mighty seventeen inchers, crashed into the city, until by the end of the war they had smashed everything to brick dust and rubble, all that is except the fantastically strong Ramparts, which were said to have been built during Napoleon's times and which held firm. In due course it became a city of the dead. It was populated only by limited numbers of troops, a few stray animals and legions of rats. Reinforcements going towards the front, or those returning from the battlefield, passed through the broken city as quickly as possible. No one loitered in the Grand Place with its all pervading smells of decay, cordite, gas, mortar dust and chloride of lime. The desolation was emphasised at night when the loneliness and emptiness of the ruins was silhouetted in the glare of flares and bursting shells." [50] Claud was to pay many visits to the stricken city, on occasion taking refuge in the Ramparts. On one occasion he brought back as souvenirs pieces of the lead tracery from the smashed stained glass windows of the Cloth Hall. [51] Ypres figured so regularly in the newspaper reports from the front that visitors were keen to see it for themselves. Mr Stratton, Director of Music of the Royal Artillery Band, which was visiting divisions at the time, was delighted when Claud took him into the city.

On the 27 October the King visited the division, lined up along the road into Reninghelst. His Majesty walked down the line and stayed for a quarter of an hour in the town square. It was an anxious

---

[50] *The Ypres Salient, Then and Now*, John Giles.

[51] I still have them.

time, for the church was well within range of the Bosch artillery. Claud was in charge of the arrangements and was reprimanded for not ensuring that the road had been swept. *Ye gods and little fishes! Quite a new role for a member of the divisional staff!*

During the first half of November Claud returned twice to Ypres, visited the 'Bluff', a spur on the north bank of the Ypres-Comines canal,[52] and the headquarters of 17th Brigade, the regular brigade, at Woodcote House on the south side of the city. In pitch darkness he met reliefs on their way out between Shrapnel Corner and the Lille Gate, and was held up in Ypres as the Bosch began to drop shells into the ruins, six HE and shrapnel landing very close to him. Later he had *a very exciting little outing* with the divisional ADMS visiting field dressing stations at Dickebusch and from there across the lake to Brasserie Farm. As they arrived at the Canadian dug-outs in Ringwood,[53] the German artillery opened fire with whizzbangs,[54] some 15 or 20 coming uncomfortably close. From Voormezeele they crossed the bridge over the canal, never a very pleasant spot, just as the Germans began shelling a nearby artillery battery. They had to make a dash for the bridge. Two shells fell very close, one just before they crossed, a second as they arrived on the opposite bank.

At the end of November the division was withdrawn to a rest area at Tilques, four miles north west of the general headquarters in St Omer. Claud was billeted on the *curé*. With two of the staff officers ill and Doyle, the AA&QMG, on leave, the arrangements for the move and billeting fell largely on Claud. Much went wrong. The days were bitterly cold with heavy frost. The gunners were caught out with no frost nails for the horses, a bridge broke, a supply column went missing whilst looking for a non-existent refilling point. Nobody was satisfied with the billets and two of the artillery brigades had to be relocated as the watering facilities were inadequate. Days of frost gave way to pouring rain. Not surprisingly Claud never went to bed before 3 am. It was with great relief that he got away for a week's well earned leave at his mother's house in Bickley.

---

[52] Now a bird sanctuary.

[53] Probably Ridgewood, according to the map.

[54] A small calibre shell.

When it was announced that Sir Douglas Haig was to relieve Sir John French as Commander-in-Chief, there was considerable relief in the BEF, not least in 24th Division. In his despatch released to the public, French had implied that it was due to the failure of the two New Army divisions that the attack at Loos had failed. The divisional staff were incensed when they found that all their letters were being opened by the censor to prevent a true account of what went wrong at the battle reaching the public at home.

Largely because of his handling of the reserves at the battle, French had lost the confidence of the BEF, including his army commanders. Quite improperly Haig was in private correspondence with the King. During the latter's visit in October, Haig had told him that French was "a source of great weakness in the army and that no-one had confidence in him any more".[55] By then French must have understood that Haig had been the cause of the libellous stories that had been circulating at home about the New Army divisions, for on 29 December Major General Capper sent a letter to all his commanding officers telling them that French, as a result of enquiries he had instigated, "has informed me personally that he was entirely satisfied that the division had done its duty well and gallantly under difficult circumstances." Claud wrote in his diary, *Hope now there will be a little less of the favouritism and that the welfare of the army in France as a whole and not that of the individual will come in for consideration. We're all fed up with the attempt of those in high places to put the blame for failures on others in the hope that personal reputations may not suffer.*

Letter from Major General Capper, to his Commanding Officer 29 December 1914

29.12.15.

My Dear ✗ ✗ ✗ ✗

I have been informed that there are still going about both in this country and at home libellous stories as to the behaviour of the 24th Division at LOOS.

I wish you to know yourself and to inform all those under your command that Field Marshal SIR JOHN FRENCH directed an enquiry to be held into the matter, and as a result of the enquiries made he informed me personally that he was entirely satisfied that the division had done its duty well and gallantly - under difficult circumstances.

I trust that all in the division will treat with the contempt it deserves the talk of scandalmongers, and be contented to know that their good conduct was appreciated by those whose opinion is really worth having.

I also hope that it will not be long before the 24th Division will have an opportunity of showing again by its conduct in the face of the enemy that the old stories were the grossest of libels.

---

[55] *The First World War*, John Keegan, p. 310.

On his return from leave to Tilques, Claud found out that the division was to relieve 49th Division, which was holding a very unpleasant length of the front north of Ypres. The roads were very bad and the mud beyond description. However, Christmas Day brought a welcome present. There had been a change of plan. The division was now to take over the line from Hooge to Bellewarde Farm astride the Menin road east of Ypres and north of the line they had held before being relieved. He had already spent three days recceing the 49th Division area and was staying at the divisional headquarters in a Trappist monastery. *The monks were very cheery and hospitable old beggars. They were not allowed to talk in the piping times of peace but during the war get dispensation. I don't think they want the war to end at all.*

During his travels he had met Paul Petrie, an Ilkley chum who commanded 11 Battery of the 4th North Riding Howitzer Brigade throughout the war and was awarded a DSO and MC. One of his men recalled Petrie's "care and devotion to his men". Its discipline, he believed, was derived "more from a sense of comradeship than from the methods normally employed by the regular army." [56]

An advanced divisional headquarters was established at Poperinghe, with the main headquarters remaining at Reninghelst. By 17 January the division had taken over its new line from Railway Wood in the north to the corner of Sanctuary Wood in the south, 17th Brigade holding the left sector, with its HQ in the Ramparts. Claud was premature in welcoming the fact that the division had not been required to take over from 49th Division, for that part of their new front from Hooge to Railway Wood had an evil reputation and was hated by the soldiers. A captain described what it was like in August 1915: "Everywhere lay the dead. The ridge in our rear was covered with dead men, their faces were blackened and swollen from three days exposure to the August sun. Haversacks, tangled heaps of webbing equipment, splintered rifles and broken stretchers lay

[56] Holmes, ibid pp. 133,134. Claud was not to know that Petrie would one day be his brother-in-law, married to my mother's sister Eileen. They lived in a beautiful house 'Ben Rhydding' on the edge of Ilkley Moors. His parent's surname was Steinthal, but he changed it to Petrie, presumably on the grounds that Steinthal sounded too German. I remember him well, a jolly, larger than life character. His elder son Tony was killed a few months before the outbreak of the Second World War when the notoriously unreliable Lysander artillery observation plane he was piloting crashed.

scattered about. The ground was pitted with shell holes of all sizes. A few solitary stakes and strands of barbed wire were all that was left of the dense mass of German entanglements. Several khaki figures were hanging on these strands in hideous attitudes. There was not a blade of grass to be seen in 'No Man's Land' or on the ridge, the ground had been completely churned up by the shells and any of the few patches of grass which had escaped had been burnt up by the liquid fire. The wood itself had suffered severely from the shell fire. Most of the trees were badly splintered and some had been torn up by the roots. There was little foliage to be seen on any of the trees. All that was left of the once bushy topped trees that lined the Menin Road were shattered stumps, and the telegraph poles stood drunkenly at all angles. Serving in the Ypres salient, one was not unaccustomed to seeing men blown to pieces and therefore I expected to see bad sights on a battlefield, but I had never expected such a dreadful and desolate sight as Hooge presented, and I never saw anything like it again during my service at the front." [57]

Phillip Gibbs, the war correspondent, wrote of Hooge, where the *château* had been destroyed early in the war by shellfire. "Afterwards there was no château but only a rubble of bricks banked up with sandbags and deep mine craters filled with stinking water slopping over from Bellewaarde Lake. Bodies and bits of bodies and clots of blood, and green, metallic-looking slime, made by explosive gases, were floating on the surface of that water below the crater banks when I first passed that way and so it always was. Human flesh, rotten and stinking, mere pulp, was pasted into the mud banks. If they dug to get deeper cover, their shovels went into the softness of dead bodies which had been their comrades. Scraps of flesh, booted legs, blackened hands, eyeless heads, came falling over them when the enemy trench-mortared their position or blew up a new mineshaft." [58]

Claud's diary records a visit to Railway Wood on 5 February. *Went up to East and West Lancs. Fine view over Bosch lines looking north east towards St Julien. Very good trenches and communication trenches good too. Lines about 40 yards apart where our front is but in front of 6th Division on our left they recede to several hundred yards in places.*

[57] John Giles, ibid, pp. 88, 89.

[58] *Realities of War*, Phillip Gibbs, quoted in John Giles, ibid p. 91.

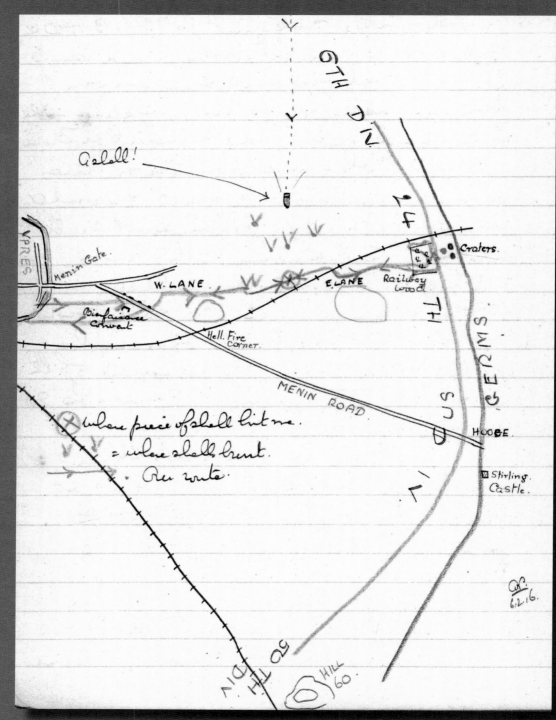

Claud's sketch map of 6 February 1916 following his visit to Railway Wood, east of Ypres

Saw flashes of guns, trains, aeroplanes, etc. Poor Handford of the East Surreys killed five or six days ago still lying out near German parapet. On our way back they were shelling East Lancs with 5.9s. We got some very close and I got a piece of shell (driving band) on the right shoulder, got me a good bang, quite enough to raise a bruise, but luckily did not penetrate. Next two or three unpleasantly close and a fair sized splinter hit a pollarded tree just between 'Dursa' and I. Back to Ypres via Bienfaisance Convent and small sally-port, crossing moat by footbridge. Tea at HQ 72nd Brigade. Home at 6 having had a very enjoyable day, not lacking in incident. Glorious sunny day. Indeed weather during last three weeks had been nothing short of marvellous for time of year. Hardly any rain at all.

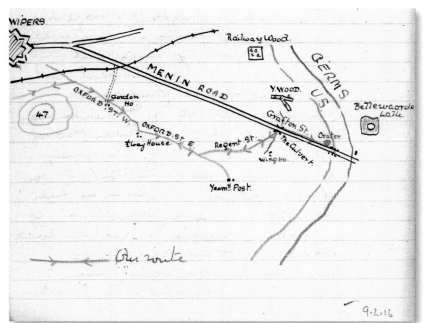

Claud's sketch map of 9 February 1916 following his visit to the front, south east of Ypres ('Wipers')

Four days later Claud went out on a trench walk to the mine crater at Hooge just behind the forward trenches, by way of Halfway House, Regent Street, and the Culvert at Grafton Street. *Hill 47 being heavily shelled as we passed. Just after leaving Halfway House it got several crumps into it. Had lunch in the crater and had only just left when 15-20 whizzbangs went straight into it. A piece got me on the right shoulder but no damage. Sniped at and nearly nabbed just later. On the way home they shelled Grafton Street and the Culvert just as we had passed. Tea with 73rd Brigade in the Ramparts. Back in car. At crossroads just west of the Asylum where Brielen road comes in, had only gone past 30 yards when two 4.2 in HE dropped just over the road. Altogether a first class day and most exciting. Weather glorious and splendid views.* The trenches at Hooge, he reported, were shockingly bad, very wet, practically no parapet in some places. The communication trenches up to the front were badly exposed and enfiladed in many places. The crater was about 25 yards across and said to be 70 feet deep and containing numerous German dead. The smell of decayed flesh was awful.

1916 was a comparatively quiet year in Flanders. Minor patrolling activity continued through the winter and the artillery was constantly engaged on defensive fire tasks. On 14/15 February the Germans carried out unexpected attacks, preceded by heavy bombardment on the Bluff in the south of the salient, Hooge and Railway Wood. Claud went out on 14 February to see how the battalions were faring and saw the start of the attack on the Bluff. *To Wipers first, then to Zillebeke dug-outs and up to Halfway House to HQ 3 Rifle Brigade. Found them all very cheerful in spite of troubles. Hay (?) went on to Culvert but they particularly asked me not to go. He found Regent Street not much damaged but Grafton Street hardly existed and was quite impassable in daylight. C5, C6 and C7 trenches were wiped out but Stables and Crater posts were still holding out. Just as we got about 50 yards from Gordon Farm they sent in a salvo of 25–30 whizzbangs at rapid fire, mostly over the farm but a few hits. We lay low and then made a dash for it and crossed in safety, the Bosch meanwhile having switched to Hellfire Corner. Just as we got to the north edge of Zillebeke Lake, Bosch opened a tremendous bombardment on to the Bluff and H trenches. For half an hour it was a regular inferno. We watched it all and could see trees being blown into the air and, I fear, trenches. Meanwhile Hooge heavily bombarded again, also vicinity of Railway Wood and many shells onto Zillebeke pond and dug-outs, Ypres Bienfaisance, etc. We had several unpleasantly close. After visiting 17th Brigade in Z dug-outs, walked across to Ypres. Got close to moat when a shrapnel burst over our heads, followed by two others. First was a very narrow shave. We crossed the moat and entered Ypres by the sally-port (not much sallying about it – we slunk in pretty quickly), just as another shell whizzed over the wall to our left. Home by car at 4.45 after a very exciting day. Dull and heavy showers and high wind.*

The attack failed to penetrate the 24th Division front. At Hooge it was mainly repulsed as a result of the gallantry of a Lewis Gun team firing from an exposed position and the excellent quick reaction of the artillery. On the Railway Wood sector the Germans exploded a mine but 9th Sussex immediately counter attacked and occupied the crater. On the right in the 17th Division sector the Germans captured most of the Bluff and the neighbouring trenches. The loss of the Bluff was a serious blow, for it overlooked a large part of the British lines. A fortnight later it was recaptured, largely as a result of a cunning artillery plan. For days and nights prior to the counter attack a

24TH DIVISION SPECIAL ORDER - NO.39.

                                    Div.H.Q.
                                    19.2.16.

          The G.O.C. Division has much pride in informing
all ranks that he has received through the Corps Commander
an expression of the Army Commander's appreciation of the
gallant conduct of the 9th Bn.ROYAL SUSSEX Regiment and the
3rd Bn.RIFLE BRIGADE during the recent fighting on the 5th
Corps front.

          The Corps Commander in forwarding this expression of
the Army Commander's appreciation congratulates these battalions on their important success.

          The G.O.C. Division desires to add to these con-
gratulations his appreciation of the conduct of the Right
Group, R.F.A. whose instant action and accurate fire mater-
ially assisted the Infantry in rendering the enemy's attack
on HOOGE abortive.

                              Cathcart.

                                    Lieut.Colonel
                                    General Staff.
                                    24th Division.

24th Division Special Order
dated 19 February 1916

60 pounder battery would fire at the Bluff at irregular intervals, stop, wait two minutes and then invariably fire another salvo. At zero hour on the day of the counter attack, 2 March, the usual salvos were fired, followed by the two minute gap. By then the German defenders had become accustomed to the pattern of the gun fire and were still crouching in their trenches waiting for the final salvo when the infantry charged. They achieved complete surprise and the Bluff was recaptured with relatively few casualties.[59] 246 Germans were taken prisoner, including 50 found in tunnels in the Bluff. Claud saw them being brought in. *They were quite a fair-looking lot, all well fed and clothed. Two or three young boys amongst them. They didn't seem very downhearted. In fact I fancy many were heartily glad to be out of the war with their lives.*

In four days of fighting, the division had lost five officers and 362 men. The divisional commander passed on the congratulations of the army and corps commanders in a special order of the day. *The old 24th is getting its tail up again, and I am glad to say we are in high favour now*, Claud told his mother.

By now the war had moved increasingly into the air with the use of aircraft not only as bombers and fighters, but also for artillery observation and reconnaissance, advising commanders of the situation with their forward troops and giving warning of preparations for an enemy counter attack. The airmen had no parachutes, though they were issued to the observers in the balloons. Initially the pilots' only armament was a rifle or pistol. Soon light machine guns were fitted but these were limited to pusher type aircraft, where the propeller was behind the pilot. In 1915 the Germans introduced a new, faster Fokker fighter able to fire forwards through the arc of the propeller as the result of an interrupter mechanism, inflicting heavy losses on the British machines. For a time they gained air superiority and the British did not regain it until the summer of 1916.[60] Claud describes an air battle over Kruisstraat. *One of our biplanes was observing for the artillery when a Fokker monoplane came along and went for the biplane. Our man tried to dive but the Bosch swooped after him like a hawk and soon got going with his machine gun. Our plane never seemed*

---

[59] Farndale, ibid p.136.

[60] Liddell Hart, ibid p, 458.

to have a look-in. Both planes came down to about 3400 feet and the biplane came down at a steep angle, falling near Shrapnel Corner. Both pilot and observer killed. The Bosch rose again very quickly and made off, our anti-aircraft guns making as usual their hopelessly indifferent shooting. It was maddening to watch and be unable to help in any way.

67

Poperinghe came under frequent attacks from German bombers. Twice in February bombs were dropped on the divisional headquarters at Reninghelst, doing little damage, though Claud could clearly hear the bombs swishing down, an uncanny noise. One bomb or possibly a dud AA shell fell beside his office without exploding. He pinned in his diary a piece of black and white canvas from a German aircraft that had been shot down.

On 21 March the division was relieved by 3rd Canadian Division, with 24th Division's headquarters moving to Fletre, three miles north west of Bailleul, undulating country relatively undamaged by shellfire. Claud lunched with the Canadian divisional commander, Major General Malcolm Mercer.[61] Claud saw two Canadian battalions, one Princess Patricia's Canadian Light Infantry, march into Reninghelst, *a fine show*. On the 28 March 24th Division took over what was to them a new sector of the front astride the River Douve from Ploegsteert Wood to the Wulverghem-Messines road, with the headquarters at St Jans Cappel. On one occasion Claud was driving through the village of Neuve Eglise (T14) when it came under shellfire. Looking back he saw a civilian shouting in evident distress about something. Thinking he might have been hit, Claud stopped the car and walked back to make sure he was alright. In fact he was merely worried about his cellar of wine, the house next door having taken a direct hit. He would not leave, so Claud advised him to take shelter in the cellar. He was walking back to the car when six 5.9 shells landed on the village in quick succession. *Had to flatten myself up against the wall and enjoyed hearing the bits fly all around. Two hit the houses just behind me, one just over the house opposite, another three 50 yards down the village. I picked up a large piece as a souvenir but dropped it pretty quick as it was red hot.*

---

[61] Mercer was killed at the Battle of Mount Sorrel in June, one of the 58 general officers who were killed or died of wounds on the Western Front. (Holmes, ibid p. 213)

Two days later Claud was visiting the forward area near Seaforth Farm (U8c) when the German artillery opened with heavy fire. *Took shelter in the dug-out of a Company HQ of 3rd Rifle Brigade and found we had selected the storm centre. We were kept prisoner for an hour, during which time about 200 shells (big 5.9 HE and shrapnel) fell within one hundred yards, twenty at least being only about forty yards off. Expected that at any minute one would fall on top of the dug-out and make some vacancies in the divisional staff. One actually did hit the dugout but luckily at the side. About six times every candle in the dug-out was blown out by the concussion. We were much amused at watching the rats being bolted out of their holes by the shelling. At such times something to attract one's attention is very helpful.*

At nearby La Plus Douce farm (T12a) Claud saw cartoons drawn by Captain Bruce Bairnsfather of the Royal Warwicks, creator of the famous 'Old Bill' character.

On 18 April divisional headquarters moved into Bailleul, which at that time was coming under frequent air attack. *About 10 to 4 am woken up by Bosch aeroplanes dropping bombs, some 15-20 in all, but nobody hurt though considerable damage to glass, roofs, doors. One fell alongside Bellingham's billet and woke him up with a start. Another amongst ambulances near Asylum, completely wrecking seven and damaging six others. This was about five yards from a house in which 160 men were sleeping. One plane hit by our AA and blown in two, coming down between Ploegsteekt and the Wood. Both pilot and observer killed.*

On 26 April Claud returned to Bickley. He declared that he had never had a more enjoyable eight days, no doubt in part because the War Office had decreed that soldiers on leave at home could wear civilian clothes. The weather had been glorious, very hot.

On 26 May, his 35th birthday, Claud celebrated with a dinner party. Doyle, the AA & QMG, brought along his brother, Sir Arthur Conan Doyle. Then 57 years old, Doyle, creator of the Sherlock Holmes stories, was said by 1920 to be one of the world's highest paid authors. As a correspondent for the *Daily Chronicle*, he had been deputed to visit the British, French and Italian fronts. Claud, who described him as *a nice old boy, very cheerful and friendly*, makes only a brief reference to the visit. *Took them up Mont Noir to see fireworks.* In his subsequent

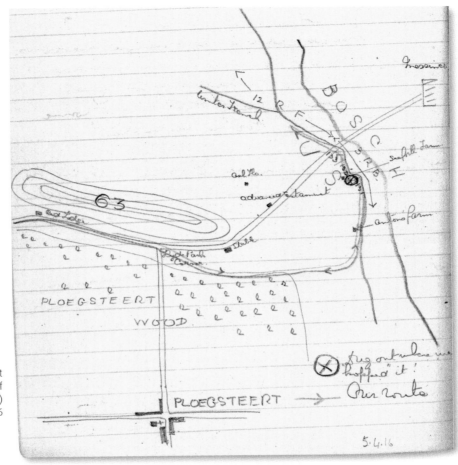

Sketch from another visit
to the front line, north of
Ploegsteert ('Plug Street')
5 April 1916

pamphlet *A Visit to Three Fronts*, published in July 1916, the author describes the evening as "one more experience of this wonderful day, the most crowded with impressions of my whole life. At night we take a car and drive north, ever north, until at a late hour we halt and climb a hill in the darkness. Below is a wonderful sight. Down on the flats, in a huge semicircle, lights are rising and falling. They are very brilliant, going for a few seconds and then dying down. Sometimes a dozen are in the air at one time. There are the dull thuds of explosions and an occasional rat-tat-tat. I have seen nothing like it, but the nearest comparison would be an enormous ten mile railway station in full swing at night with signals winking, lamps waving, engines hissing and carriages bumping. It is a terrible place down yonder which will live as long as military history is written, for it is the Ypres salient. What a salient it is too! A huge curve, as outlined by the lights, needing only a little more to be an encirclement. Something caught the rope as it closed and that something was the British soldier. But it is a perilous place still by day and by night. Never shall I forget the ceaseless, malignant activity which was borne in upon me by the white, winking lights, the red sudden glares and the horrible thudding noises in that place of death beneath me.[62]

An earlier visitor to the headquarters in January had been the Duke D'Urcal, a descendant of a branch of the Spanish Royal Family. Comte de Pret, the Belgian liaison officer with 24th Division, had brought him to lunch.

An unexpected party had turned up two days before Conan Doyle's visit. Four Royal Naval officers and 52 ratings had come to spend five days in the trenches *just to see what's going on. They are keen as mustard and awfully keen to see a show. In fact units find it somewhat difficult to curb their enthusiasm in the trenches.*

All through June and into July Claud was fully committed to what he described to his mother as *a special reconnaissance job.* It involved going out on foot every day, checking on road conditions and selecting billets for troops and transport and watering facilities for the horses in an area east and south east of Kemmel Hill. Fortunately for the most part the weather was excellent, almost too hot. Some of the roads were so cut up by shell fire and old trenches and overgrown with grass and weeds that they were barely recognisable as such. It was interesting work. He was enjoying the opportunity to be out in the open day after day. With all the walking he was losing weight, his feet were becoming sore, he was sunburnt and he was *getting quite decently slim again.* At times the work was exciting. From Kemmel Hill on 2 June he saw the German artillery open an intense straffe prior to an attack on the Canadian division at Mount Sorrel and Hooge. The attack was preceded by the explosion of four mines and met with considerable success. By late afternoon the Germans had gained ground 700 yards west of their start line and had captured Mount Sorrel and much of Armagh and Sanctuary Woods. Ten days later the Canadians mounted an operation to

---

[62] *A Visit to Three Fronts*, Sir Arthur Conan Doyle.

recover the lost ground. The initial barrage was so intense that German resistance was overwhelmed. Within an hour the battle was over and the Canadians had recovered all the ground they had lost.

On 11 June Claud was out visiting the OP on Kemmel Hill and was just leaving *when the Bosche began to send over some 4.2s. First two which fell about 50 yards off were luckily duds. Next two much better and we prostrated ourselves on the ground. I found my face in a puddle and got my nose dirty. Several more came along pretty close and we found urgent work to do down the hill.*

There is no explanation in the diary about the purpose of what he refers to as his *magnum opus*. It was probably dictated by Haig's plan to use the ANZAC Corps to open an attack towards Messines if the offensive on the Somme should fail. To this end two brigades of 24th Division were relieved by 2nd Australian Division. News of the great push on 1 July reached the staff of 24th Division slowly and piecemeal. The diary makes no mention of the appalling casualties, but when on 6 July reports were received that the army in the south was "consolidating", it was apparent to Claud that *the offensive is at a standstill, at least for the time being.* The following day orders were received that the ANZAC Corps was to move south, there to take part in the bloody battle for Pozieres. *Suppose our show up here now off and all my hours and days of work were for nought.* There was, however, some consolation. Claud had read in the *London Gazette* that he had been awarded a DSO in the King's Birthday Honours. His reaction was typical. *I suppose it is all very nice, but I can't help feeling that staff officers are amply recompensed for a certain amount of hard work by their emoluments and comparative comfort, and I feel that awards like the DSO should be reserved for the poor fellows who have to stick the continual dangers and discomforts of the front line trenches.* He was too modest. His Herculean effort in putting the division back on its feet following the disaster of Loos was more than reason enough.[63]

On 19 July orders were received that 24th Division was to leave Flanders at last and deploy to the Somme.

---

[63]   In addition to the DSO, he was Mentioned-in-Despatches five times: 22 January 1915; 25 June 1916; 15 May 1917; 21 May 1918; and 22 December 1918.

SPECIAL ORDER OF THE DAY

BY

GENERAL SIR DOUGLAS HAIG,

G.C.B., K.C.I.E., K.C.V.O., A.D.C.

Commander-in-Chief, British Armies in France.

It is with deep regret that I communicate to the Armies in France the following telegram received from the War Office.

D. Haig. Genl.

General Headquarters,
7th June, 1916.

Commanding-in-Chief,
British Armies in France.

GENERAL SIR DOUGLAS HAIG,

GENERAL HEADQUARTERS, FRANCE.

6th June.

By His Majesty's commands the following order has been issued to the Army. The King has learned with profound regret of the disaster by which the Secretary of State for War has lost his life while proceeding on a special mission to the Emperor of Russia. Field-Marshal Lord Kitchener gave 45 years of distinguished service to the State, and it is largely due to his administrative genius and unwearying energy that the Country has been able to create and place in the field the Armies which are to-day upholding the traditional glories of our Empire. Lord Kitchener will be mourned by the Army as a great Soldier who under conditions of unexampled difficulty rendered supreme and devoted service both to the Army and the State.

By Command of the Army Council,

R. H. BRADE.

STATIONERY SERVICES PRESS A—6/16.

Special Order of the Day by the Commander-in-Chief dated 7 June 1916 announcing the death of Field Marshal Lord Kitchener

h1>Chapter 6   ON THE SOMME
23 July – 19 November 1916</h1>

When Claud set out on 23 July to drive 80 miles to Amiens, he was entering a very different landscape from the flat lands and drainage ditches of Flanders to the rolling chalk downs, small villages, copses and dense woods of the Somme. This is beautiful country now, surprisingly under-populated. At its centre is the small, bustling town of Albert, where the farmers bring their produce to sell at the market stalls in the square. It is also a countryside of hundreds of thousands of soldiers' graves.

In moving south 24th Division's role was to reinforce Rawlinson's Fourth Army. The army was composed initially of 20 divisions, half of them from Kitchener's New Army, some, such as the 36th (Ulster) Division and the South Africans, seeing action for the first time. Flanders had been relatively quiet that summer and 24th Division had had an uneventful war since the *débacle* of Loos. Now, as they travelled southwards in military trains, they were about to be drawn into an intense battle that had been raging since the beginning of the month.

After the failure of the 'big push' on Thiepval, the main thrust of the battle had concentrated on the south side of the old Roman road from Albert to Bapaume. In a series of attacks that had resulted in appalling casualties on both sides, Fourth Army had failed to achieve a break through.

74

By now the countryside had been devastated as the British and German artillery fought to dominate the battlefield. The British seldom expended fewer than a million rounds in a week, more than the total it had fired in the first six months of the war.[64] Directing the main weight of their fire on counter battery tasks, the British were winning the contest.

Claud drove south by way of Béthune, St Poll and Doullens. The day was very hot and *the dust too awful for words. The car went splendidly with no sort of accidents.* Evidently he still did not entirely trust these relatively newfangled machines. He spent the night at the Belfort Hotel in Amiens. For the next two days he was extremely busy. The corps staff were not much help. He was working until 3 am on the second day, 6 am on the next, arranging billets and meeting trains arriving at stations on the outskirts of Amiens. Some of the units had marches of up to 17 miles to their billeting areas, bivouacking overnight. There was a good deal of grousing. The area between Amiens and Albert had been transformed into an enormous military encampment, cut by new roads leading to the front and covered with shell dumps, gun positions and camps.[65] By 26 July the division was concentrated in an assembly area. Claud went to bed at 8.30 pm and slept until 9 am the following day.

Propgramme for a concert party given by 7th Battalion The Northamptonshire Regiment on 28 July 1916, which Claud attended.

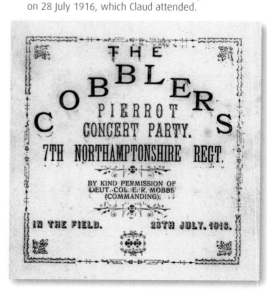

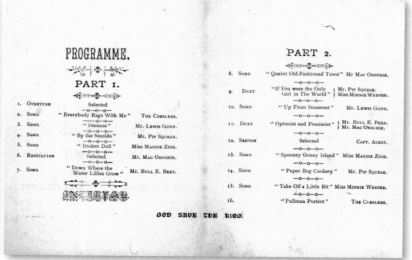

---

[64] Holmes, ibid p.42.

[65] Keegan, ibid p.312.

Five days later the division was detailed as reserve to XIII Corps and moved forward by bus, military train and on foot to the area between the Somme and the Ancre, with divisional headquarters at Corbie at the confluence of the two rivers. Claud had *a lovely billet at 20 Place de la République. Very nice hosts.* But it was not to last. On 2 August they moved further east, with the headquarters at Citadel Camp, near Fricourt.[66] The accommodation was rudimentary and infested with rats and flies, but some of it at least was in huts, despite being well within the range of the German guns. It was difficult to sleep because, after the long dry summer, the ground was very hard[67] and because of the tremendous noise of the incessant firing of the guns on both sides. A howitzer down the valley *makes a noise like a hiccup and is very trying*, he told his mother. A chance shell at midnight hit a French ammunition dump. *It went off like a Brocks Benefit. The grand finale when the rockets went up was particularly fine.*

During the next nine days, whilst the division waited for orders to move, Claud walked and rode over the battlefields of the first half of July. At Mametz, where the Welsh Division had lost a quarter of its strength in an attack on the wood, he walked along the original German first line and marvelled at the dugouts *a wonderful monument to Bosch industry*. They had taken advantage of the lack of fighting since the early days of the war on the Somme to build an elaborate network of dugouts 30 feet under the hard chalk downs, impervious to artillery fire, behind barbed wire entanglements supported by machine gun nests and interconnected with telephone cables between dugouts and running to the rear. Some even had home comforts such as wallpaper.

At Fricourt Claud saw some of the massive mine craters tunnelled under the German lines by the sapper tunnelling companies and blown simultaneously at zero hour on 1 July, explosions so huge that they were heard across the Channel, even in London. The craters are still there. The mine at Lochnagar, adjacent to La Boisselle, left a crater 90 yards across and 70 feet deep. Each year on the anniversary the bottom is strewn with a carpet of British Legion poppies.

---

[66] Holmes, ibid p.281 states that by November it was a hutted camp.

[67] A few days later he persuaded the sappers to make him a camp bed.

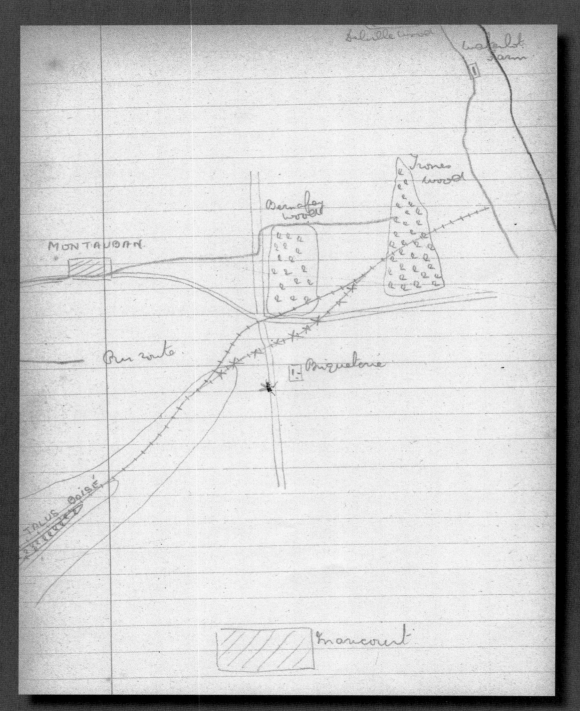

Sketch map showing Claud's route through Montauban to Trones Wood on 10 August 1916

Three days later the King visited the craters. Claud described the visit to his mother. *I got a very good view of him in his car. He looked awfully well and very cheery. He stayed about two hours on the old Bosch line. I must say he ran a by no means inconsiderable risk as on the very next day, and on several days afterwards, the Bosch put black crumps on the very spot where the Royal party had stood.*

On 11 August, two of the brigades, the 17th Brigade and 72nd Brigade, deployed into the front line from Delville Wood via Waterlot Farm to Arrow Head Copse, facing Guillemont. That day Claud and two companions walked up to Bernafay Wood and then on to Trones Wood. The Germans were shelling Trones. *We had two* [shells] *uncomfortably near, notably one only about 20 yards away which was fortunately a dud. Too hot to go walking about, so we went to lunch at the Advanced Dressing Station in Bernafay Wood. Afterwards we walked again into Trones Wood in fear and trembling as the Huns were putting stuff all around, especially big black HEs in the south west corner. A lot of our dead and the Bosch lying around. We must try and make some effort to bury them.* But that was hazardous work, as he explains in his next letter. *I picked up a Bosch revolver yesterday but handed it over to a Royal Fusiliers subaltern as I did not want to keep it, even if I was allowed to. I also got a brass cartridge case of a big German howitzer which makes a nice trophy.[68] There are hundreds of them lying about. The amount of rifles, kits, rations, ammunition and other various flotsam and jetsam of the battlefield is amazing and makes one almost weep when you realise that the war is costing about £6,000,000 a day! Of course we are doing all we can to "salve" things but it can only go along slowly. Shortage of labour and the Bosch guns both hinder one considerably.*

The division went into action for the first time since arriving on the Somme front, on the night 16/17 August when 9th East Surreys made an attack on enemy trenches between Arrow Head Copse and Guillemont. As Keegan writes: "The Somme was becoming an arena of attrition to which fresh divisions were sent in monotonous succession, only to waste their energy in bloody struggles for tiny patches of ground." [69] Liddell Hart described the ground over which

---

[68] I think I have the base, stamped 'Magdeburg 1915'.

[69] Keegan, ibid p.319.

the East Surreys made their attack. "From Trones Wood it is down one slope, up another, only a few hundred yards of farm road, yet in July and August an infinite distance. Division after division essayed to cross it, felt the petty prize within their fingers and then slipped back, unable to maintain their hold." [70]

The East Surreys attack failed, gaining about 300 yards of ground at heavy cost, *nine officers and about 150*, Claud recorded. He visited the brigade next day, east of Talus Boise, then up to the Briquetterie and Bernafay Wood. Next night 8th Queens tried to take the same strong-point and also failed. That afternoon XIII Corps, XIV Corps and the French Corps on the right flank of the British line mounted a concerted attack. Claud watched it from high ground near Minden Post, south east of Mametz. *Bombardment a regular inferno. Saw some of our fellows go over the top and forward. With a few exceptions the whole affair seems to have been a great success. 14th Division got objectives (less NE corner of Delville Wood) almost at once and some hundreds of prisoners and some mgs. In our division 17th Brigade got objectives (including the station at Guillemont[71]) almost at once, probably about 200 prisoners in 73rd Brigade. 7th Northants got objectives, but Middlesex and Leinsters were driven back by same strong-point. French did splendidly. Have now the whole of Maurepas and ravine beyond and many prisoners. Fear our losses heavy, especially in Northants, Middlesex and Leinsters.*

That evening Claud visited the prisoners' cage. *Not very full. Only one officer and about a dozen other ranks*, he described them in his letter on 24 August. By then the division had been withdrawn into a rest area in the neighbourhood of the Citadel. *The prisoners I saw were on the whole of very good stamp, well set up and fed, but they seem very much shaken. Our fellows are extremely good to them and treat them with great consideration.* In the same letter Claud asked his mother to send him wool and cotton thread and darning needles, so that his servant could mend his clothes. Also two sticks of Colgate shaving soap, a half pound of Army and Navy Smoking Mixture No 2 for himself and two pounds of sugar lumps for his horse, Sandy.

---

[70] Liddell Hart, ibid p.327.

[71] Claud's sketches show a light railway running out to Guillemont.

After two days in the rest area, the division moved into camps on the downs above Morlancourt, with the headquarters at Buire on the Ancre. On 26 August he had spent the day riding round the brigade areas. On his return he was greeted with the news that he was posted forthwith to 31st Division as AA&QMG in the temporary rank of lieutenant colonel. He was jubilant. *Temporary rank of Lt Col*, he told his mother *not bad, he, what? Fat old Colonel now! Very good thing to get a rise, especially at my age* [he was 35]. *Awfully sorry to leave the Division as I am now the oldest member of the staff with one exception. The white heather* [sent by his mother and still with her letters] *seems to have brought me luck at once.*

Claud was dined out of the divisional mess that night. The following morning he set out to drive northwards to 31st Division headquarters at Lestrem, seven miles north east of Bethune, which by then had been heavily shelled. He took the opportunity to make a short detour to visit his 1914 gun position at Le Touret. It was still the same. Many of the houses in the village had completely disappeared but his old billet still stood, with the same toothless old woman living in it. On arrival at the divisional headquarters he found he was not expected and no-one knew anything about him. Neither did corps and army headquarters. Eventually he was able to ascertain from GHQ that there was a mistake in the signal posting him to 31st Division. It should have read 41st Division. He retraced his steps, spent the night in a hotel in Doullens and finally arrived at the headquarters of the correct division the following morning.

Claud found the HQ out of the line resting at Ailly-le-Haut-Clocher, six miles south east of Abbeville. His horses Sandy and Builloo arrived the following day, which says much for the military railway system.[72] He settled quickly into his new appointment. He liked the divisional commander, General Lawford.[73] His predecessor as AA & QMG *seems to have done nothing in the way of running the show*

---

[72] 41st Division had been raised in October 1915, made up of Pals battalions from various parts of the UK. It arrived in France in May 1916 and was now about to take part in its first major engagement, the Battle of Flers-Courcellette. Its three brigades were 122nd, 123rd and 124th.

[73] General Sir Sidney Lawford's son, Peter, became a Hollywood film star, a member of Frank Sinatra's notorious 'Rat Pack'. In 1954 he married Patricia Kennedy, daughter of Joseph Kennedy and sister of John F Kennedy.

but left everything to his deputies. Luckily two excellent men under me, Major Holmes à Court and Captain White. He rode round the rest area visiting the administrative units and the gunners, the latter at Pont Remy on the Somme, where they were billeted in a fine *château*, said to have been the English headquarters before Crécy and occupied by the German general staff during the fighting at the Somme in the Franco-Prussian war of 1870.

The division was passing the time holding a horse show. Claud took part in the tent-pegging but was out of practice and scored only two touches. Sandy, perhaps too full of sugar lumps, refused to jump and had to be left out of the competitions.

The next day, 4 September, the division received orders to join XV Corps in the neighbourhood of Dernancourt in the Ancre valley south west of Albert. Claud drove down the same day to recce the area. It was a miserable journey, the hood leaked and they lost their way, arriving back at the divisional headquarters *somewhat subdued in spirit!* He had called in *en route* to visit his old division, 24th Division, and found it had suffered heavy casualties in recent days. Two of his close friends, Brigadier General Philpotts and his brigade major, had been killed. "So much for senior officers being safe," Holmes comments.[74]

Over the following week the brigades arrived by train and vehicles, 123rd Brigade taking over the line in front of Delville Wood, the other two in camps at Fricourt and Becordel. The following day, 12 September, they began to move into their battle positions in York Valley just south of Longueval. Two days later he recorded, *Round Brigade HQs (122 and 124) in York Trench and visited dumps. Our guns giving the Hun a fine dose, his reply feeble. Saw the new Tanks. Hope they will be a great success.* [He told his mother they were like great whales. The tommies referred to them as 'the Irish Navy'.] *Traffic on roads awful. Took us nearly three hours to get back from Montauban. (only four miles). Masses of cavalry (three or four divisions, or so I am told). Feeling a bit off colour, with head and fever. Have had a very busy week, but think everything is now ready for great day.*

---

[74] Holmes, ibid p.47.

The battle of the Somme was getting nowhere. Limited Allied advances at fearful cost in casualties were beaten back by counter attacks, equally costly to the German defenders. Now Haig decided it might be possible to end the stalemate by using the tanks to break through the German third line, the last of the elaborately constructed lines still in their hands.

The existence of the tanks was a well kept secret. The Germans seem to have had no warning that they were about to appear on the battlefield. Of the 60 machines already in France, 49 were available for the attack, of which 32 reached the start line. Against the advice of their progenitor, a young sapper officer, Colonel Ernest Swinton, they were about to be deployed in small groups of fewer than half a dozen rather than *en masse*.

The offensive was to be mounted by the Reserve Army on the left, Fourth Army at the centre composed of III, XIV and XV Corps, with the French on the right. Over the three previous days an enormous weight of fire was brought down on the enemy gun positions with 56 guns and howitzers allocated to counter battery targets directed from the air. The pilots came under little opposition. By now the Allies had gained air superiority.

Zero hour was 6.30 am. The infantry advanced behind the recently developed and highly successful creeping barrage, in which lanes had been left for the advancing tanks. On the left the attack was not wholly successful, in part because the corps commander had insisted on his tanks advancing through High Wood, with the result that three of the four tanks became ditched. On the right the attack failed, but at the centre, on the XV Corps front, the tanks came into their own. When the advance faltered at the entrance to Flers, four tanks drove up the main street, which had not been much damaged, followed by the cheering infantry.[75] Infantry and tanks together pushed on beyond Flers to Gueudecourt, their final objective. The village was beyond the range of the 18 pounders. The batteries galloping forward over ground pockmarked by shell holes and exposed to rifle and machine gun fire from the village, suffered heavily. The defenders, though their morale had been badly shaken

---

[75] A memorial now stands looking down the street along which they advanced.

by the sudden appearance of the tanks, with many reports of them running away from their positions, were still able to mount counter attacks, driving the British back to Flers, but the village remained in 41st Division's hands. A huge bite had been taken out of the original German reserve line. The cost had been heavy, 30,000 in Fourth Army. Six commanding officers were killed or wounded. [76]

Haig, delighted with the success of the tanks, ordered another thousand to be manufactured. In his congratulatory message to Rawlinson, he wrote: "Our main engine of war, the 'Heavy Section of the Machine Gun Corps' [the code name for the tanks] acquitted itself splendidly in its first trial and has proved a very valuable addition to the Army." How much more might they have accomplished if they had been used *en masse*. [77]

The next day Claud and a companion attempted to walk over the battlefield to Flers. Starting from Longueval, they followed the Flers road to Switch Trench. The trench and surrounding area were piled up with German and British dead. Heavy German shellfire, shrapnel and 5.9 HE, prevented them reaching the village. From Switch Trench and the church tower in Longueval, they could see the Germans removing guns. There were derelict tanks all over the place, one on fire west of Gueudecourt, the limit of the 41st Division attack. The forward batteries were coming under heavy fire. They retraced their steps through Delville Wood. [78] He concluded the diary entry, *Lovely day*.

[76] One of the COs killed was Lieutenant Colonel Charles Duncombe, Earl of Faversham, who died whilst leading the battalion he had raised into its first battle, 21st KRRC. He lies in the Grass Lane Cemetery at Flers, along with his pet deerhound. (Holmes, ibid p.627). It was not unusual for pets to accompany their masters to war.

[77] The Germans did not develop a tank until 1918, much inferior to the British model.

[78] Delville Wood and the neighbouring High Wood were two dense woods that dominated the approach from the south west, providing ideal cover for the defenders. Not without reason it earned the nickname 'Devil's Wood'. In an attack two months earlier the South African division, going into action for the first time, had been almost wiped out, just 143 surviving unscathed. It was finally taken on 29 July after an intense barrage had set the trees on fire. The author and war correspondent Phillip Gibbs gave a graphic description of the wood at the end of July: "The German soldiers have the advantage in the defence. They have placed their machine guns behind barricades of great tree trunks, hidden their sharpshooters up in the foliage of trees, still standing above all the litter of branches smashed down by shrapnel and high explosive, and send a patter of . . .

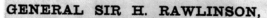

GENERAL SIR H. RAWLINSON,
COMMANDING FOURTH ARMY.

O.A.D. 151. *17th September.* 1916.

The great successes won by the Fourth Army on the 15th are most satisfactory and have brought us another long step forward towards the final victory. The further advance yesterday after such severe fighting was also a fine performance highly creditable to the troops and to Corps, Divisional and Brigade Staffs. Our new engine of war, the heavy Section Machine Gun Corps acquitted itself splendidly on its first trial and has proved itself a very valuable addition to the Army. My warmest congratulations to you and the Fourth Army on a very fine achievement.

D. Haig. Genl.

Commanding-in-Chief,
British Armies in France.

ARMY PRINTING AND STATIONERY SERVICES A—9/16.

Congratulatory Order from the Commander-in-Chief, General Sir Douglas Haig, sent to the 4th Army, 17 September 1916

The following day they set out again to see how the clearance of the battlefield was progressing. They checked on the forward dumps, then on to Longueval through Delville Wood where the burial and salvage parties had had to withdraw under heavy shellfire. There were a good many casualties along the Flers Road, mainly in the teams taking up gun ammunition to the forward batteries.

---

[78] *continued* . . . bullets across to our men who have dug holes for themselves below the tough roots… There were not two yards without a shell hole. Fallen trees and brushwood made a tangled maze. Old barricades smashed by shellfire and shallow trenches scraped out by men digging their own graves at the same time made obstacles and pitfalls everywhere." *The Battle of the Somme*, Phillip Gibbs, pp.143 and 149.

SPECIAL ORDER OF THE DAY
By
GENERAL SIR DOUGLAS HAIG,
G.C.B., G.C.V.O., K.C.I.E., A.D.C.
Commander-in-Chief, British Armies in France.

The following letters are published for the information of all ranks :—

To GENERAL SIR DOUGLAS HAIG.

(Translation).

G.H.Q. OF FRENCH ARMIES,
17th September, 1916.

MY DEAR GENERAL,

I desire to convey to you my most sincere congratulations on the brilliant successes gained by the British troops under your command during the hard-fought battles of the 15th and 16th of September. Following on the continuous progress made by your armies since the beginning of the Somme offensive, these fresh successes are a sure guarantee of final victory over our common enemy, whose physical and moral forces are already severely shaken.

Permit me, my dear General, to take this opportunity of saying that the combined offensive which we have carried on now for more than two months has, if it were possible, drawn still closer the ties which unite our two Armies—our adversary will find therein proof of our firm determination to combine our efforts until the end, to ensure the complete triumph of our cause.

I bow before those of your soldiers by whose bravery these successes have been achieved, but who have fallen before the completion of our task ; and I ask you to convey, in my name and in the name of the whole French Army, to those who stand ready for the fights still to come, a greeting of comradeship and confidence.

(Signed)   J. JOFFRE.

To GENERAL JOFFRE.

GENERAL HEADQUARTERS,
BRITISH ARMIES IN FRANCE,
19th September, 1916.

MY DEAR GENERAL,

I thank you most sincerely for the kind message of congratulation and goodwill that you have addressed to me and to the troops under my command on their recent successes. This fresh expression of the good wishes of yourself and of your gallant Army, without whose close co-operation and support those successes could scarcely have been achieved, will be very warmly appreciated by all ranks of the British Armies.

I thank you, too, for your noble tribute to those who have fallen. Our brave dead, whose blood has been shed together on the soil of your great country, will prove a bond to unite our two peoples long after the combined action of our Armies has carried the common cause for which they have fought to its ultimate triumph.

The unremitting efforts of our forces north and south of the Somme, added to the glorious deeds of your Armies unaided at Verdun, have already begun to break down the enemy's powers of resistance ; while the energy of our troops and their confidence in each other increases from day to day. Every fresh success that attends our arms brings us nearer to the final victory to which, like you, I look forward with absolute confidence.

Yours very truly,
(Signed)   D. HAIG, GENERAL.

On 18 September the division came out of the line to a rest area near Albert, with the headquarters in Ribemont on the Ancre. The long hot days of the summer, when the ground had been baked so hard that Claud found it an uncomfortable bed, had ended. The autumn rains had come early. He spent two days trying to sort out the camps, eventually procuring shelters and persuading the sappers to provide tarpaulins. Then it was a matter of finding baths in Amiens for the troops, a task (like the camps) that should have been carried out by the corps staff. For the first time in a fortnight he wrote to his mother, *I have been so busy of late that I have not had any time for letter writing. I am at it all day and late into the night. However, the troops have got to be equipped and fed and somebody has to do it. A week of absolute swine-hog weather, pouring with rain and very cold. It is very hard on our poor infantry who had nothing but a bivouac shelter to lie under. However, a little sun soon puts them right and they are now as keen as mustard to have another go at the Hun.*

The division was still out of the line when the battle was renewed on 25 September. XV Corps, supported by one or two tanks, captured Gueudecourt, whilst the French on the right occupied Combles, and on the left Gough's reserve army, supported by three tanks, at last captured Thiepval, taking one thousand prisoners.

The division returned to the line on 4 October, with one brigade just west of Gueudecourt and the divisional headquarters in Fricourt Château, or what there was left of it. All that remained was a heap of bricks in a wilderness of shell holes, old trenches and *débris* from the prolonged bombardment. Claud had a room in the cellars, cold and damp, with *fine fat rats* that had thrived for weeks in the shelled *château* graveyard. When it rained, and it seldom seemed to stop, water flooded down the steps and into the cellar. Claud used buckets to bale it out, *otherwise I would have had to swim*. The divisional offices were in old German dugouts, *regular underground houses, like being on the lower deck of a ship*.

During the next three days, Claud went round the three brigades by motor and walking, by way of Mametz, Bernafay and Longueval. The mud made walking difficult, whilst the roads were well nigh impassable. The Germans were shelling the rear areas. He had another near miss when a 5.9 detonated so close that it blew his walking stick out of his hand.

The attack on 7 October mounted by the three corps and the French was met by heavy machine gun fire, much of it at long range, and was beaten back. 41st Division had advanced only 150 yards and lost 1,200 men. All next day the rain poured down. There were extreme difficulties in carrying back the wounded over long distances through the mud.

By mid October Haig had come to realise that there was little hope of effecting a breakthrough, but under pressure from Foch he persisted with costly attacks until the Germans had withdrawn to their original third line stretching from Transloy to in front of Bapaume. Lord Cavan *our distinguished cousin*, who had thanked Claud for his battery's fire support in 1914, and was now a lieutenant general commanding XIV Corps, protested that any further attempts to advance would only end in failure and pointless sacrifice. Day after day of rain, the barrages of the artillery had turned the ground into a quagmire. The chalky soil of the Somme landscape is glutinous, clinging to boots until they seem twice as heavy. Guns sank into the mud. Sometimes it took 10 to 12 hours to manhandle a single 18 pounder forward to maintain fire support for the infantry advances towards Transloy ridge. Ammunition had to be dragged forward on corrugated iron sledges.[79] In places trenches were three to four feet deep in mud. There was no shelter from the rain. Claud was lucky to be able to sleep in his cellar under Fricourt Château, though one night he had woken to find his bedclothes soaked in dew, his feet so numb with cold that he could not struggle up to put on a pair of wet socks.

In mid November there was one more major attack, when the reserve army on the left flank captured Beaumont Hamel and took 7,000 prisoners. It was the last act in the tragedy of the Somme. On 19 November the battle was officially brought to an end. The furthest point of the advance was seven miles on from the front on 1 July. "Those few miles had cost the Allies 600,000 casualties, the Germans a similar number. To the British it [the Somme] would remain the greatest military tragedy of the 20th century, indeed of their national military history. The regiments of Pals and Chums, which had their first experience of war on the Somme, have been

---

[79] Farndale, ibid p.154.

called an army of innocents, and that, in their readiness to offer up their lives in circumstances none had anticipated in their heady days of volunteering, it undoubtedly was. The Somme marked the end of an age of vital optimism in British life that has never been recovered." [80]

"Memories of the Somme," Farndale wrote, "are of a long drawn out jumbled nightmare of mud, wet, death, faulty equipment, faulty ammunition, untrained reinforcements, precarious communications, constant enemy shelling, mud, mud, mud and terrible exhaustion." [81]

41st Division had long since left the area. On 12 October it had been withdrawn to a rest area around Hellencourt, north east of Abbeville, for a badly needed break. *I'm getting a bit stale*, Claud admitted. *Brain not quite clear at times. I look forward to leave being reopened some day and long for a really good loaf for ten days.*

Four days later they set off north eastwards, back to the Ypres sector. Rawlinson regretted losing them. In a warm letter, he concluded, "I trust that some time in the future it may be my good fortune to have this fine division again in the Fourth Army."

Fourth Army No. 335 (G.S.)

41st Division.

I desire to place on record my appreciation of the work done by the 41st Division during the Battle of the Somme and to congratulate all ranks on the brilliant manner in which they captured the village of FLERS on September 15th. To assault three lines of strongly defended trench systems, and to capture the village of FLERS as well, in one rush was a feat of arms of which every officer, non-commissioned officer and man may feel proud.

It was a very fine performance and I offer my best thanks for the gallantry and endurance displayed by all ranks.

The work of the Divisional Artillery in supporting the infantry attacks and in establishing the barrages deserves high praise, and I trust that at some future time it may be my good fortune to have this fine Division again in the Fourth Army.

H.Q., Fourth Army,
27th October, 1916.

General,
Commanding Fourth Army.

Congratulatory letter from Commander Fourth Army to the 41st Division following their capture of the village of Flers on 15 September 1916.

---

[80] Keegan, ibid p.321.

[81] Farndale, ibid p.156.

Chapter 7   **THE BATTLE OF MESSINES**
                     October 1916 – July 1917

Whilst the battles raged in the south, the Flanders front held by
Plumer's Second Army had been very quiet. In mid November,
41st Division took over the lines on the St Eloi sector from the Ypres-
Comines canal to the Bois de Carée, whilst the divisional headquarters
moved into new huts in Reninghelst, six miles to the rear.
When Claud carried out an inspection of the rear area with the
GOC, they found the camps in a very bad state. Practically nothing
had been done to prepare for the winter. The front line was lightly
held with one brigade manning the trenches, the second in support,
the third at rest in the rear, the brigades rotating every four days.
The trenches had been allowed to deteriorate and were in a poor
state of repair. In the last days of October when there was heavy rain,
they became waterlogged. It was impossible to excavate dugouts.
There was an all-pervading stench of rotting bodies, uniforms
became infested with lice and rats grew fat on the dead.

The winter of 1917 was exceptionally harsh, the worst in living
memory across Europe. At Ypres a temperature was recorded of –20°
Fahrenheit. For a month it never rose above freezing. At least the
frozen ground made movement easier, but when it thawed the mud
returned. The last heavy snowfall was on 23 March, but there was still
snow in April. Conditions for the soldiers in the line were appalling.
As a result of standing for long periods in flooded trenches, they
developed trench foot, their feet turning blue and darkening and
liable to become gangrenous. Not that life in the huts, now built in

the rear areas, was much better. They were bare and draughty, with a shortage of fuel to keep the stoves burning.

From the first Claud appreciated that something had to be done to ensure that at least the brigades at rest had a chance to get clean and relax in more civilised surroundings. He was responsible for the divisional bath house where their clothes were laundered and deloused, a complete set of underwear was issued and every man got a hot bath about once a week. Claud was responsible for the 240 local girls who ran the baths, *some of them pretty unruly. All sorts of questions came up before me, some of them somewhat embarrassing.* At the height of the freeze in February, all the pipes and boilers froze and burst.

Claud's other project which gave him a great deal of satisfaction was the setting up of a tea and supper room where the men could relax in comfort and purchase a meal at half the price of the *estaminets* in the town. He described it in one of his letters. *The tea room is very nicely got up and provides the men with a first class tea with fancy pastries, ham sandwiches, etc, for 50 centimes a head, brought to them by fair haired Belgian damsels with nice neat white aprons with our divisional sign on them. From 3 to 5.30 there is a constant stream coming and going, every seat in the room taken. From 6.30 to 8.30 they get suppers, liver and bacon, sausages and mash, rissoles, etc.*

The following day Claud's other pet project opened – the divisional theatre. The first performance was booked out days in advance. The Pierrot Troupe formed from talent within the division and called 'Crumps' was of a high standard. The programme would have included the wistful songs of wartime: *Roses of Picardy; Keep the Home Fires Burning;* and *There's a Long, Long Trail A-Winding.* In after years it was the last song that always reminded Claud most poignantly of all the friends he had lost.

There were facilities to show silent films; Charlie Chaplin was a particular favourite. An early patron was Plumer, the army commander. In April there was a gala performance in aid of the Belgian Red Cross in the presence of the Queen of the Belgians, accompanied by her son, Prince Leopold, and Prince Alexander of Teck. After the performance there was a dinner in the divisional mess. The Queen was charming and evidently enjoyed herself.

90

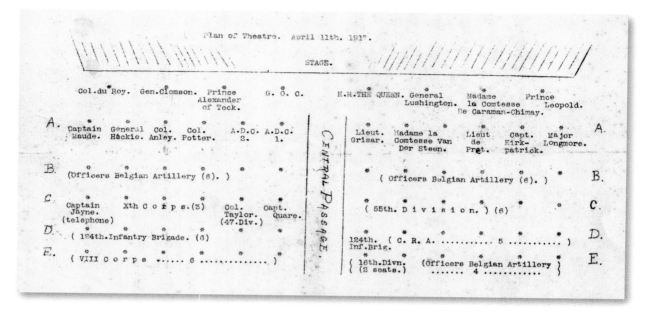

The seating plan for the gala concert in aid of the Belgian Red Cross held on the evening of 11 April 1917

Four days before Christmas, the Commander-in-Chief, the newly promoted Field Marshal Sir Douglas Haig, visited the division, including the divisional battle school. He spoke highly of the reputation of the 41st Division. Claud, who was introduced to him, described him to his mother. *He looked very fit and well and has a very fine face, essentially that of a strong man.* That evening, after the Commander-in-Chief had departed, the corps commander was invited to Christmas dinner in the mess. Pride of place on the menu was given to the plum pudding cooked by Isobel, his mother's cook back in Bickley. Claud asked her to tell Isobel that it had been particularly praised by the assembled company, including no fewer than three generals, but there had been some disappointment that there was no sixpence inside. In her next letter his mother assured him there had indeed been a sixpence. Claud wondered which general had swallowed it.

Claud's numerous tasks in the divisional rear area and at the headquarters, including checks on the advanced dressing and casualty clearance stations and ammunition dumps, visiting the artillery wagon lines to check on stabling for the horses, left him with less time to visit the battalions and curtailed the battlefield walks he had been accustomed to take in the past. His diary records one such visit to the front line on the first day of the New Year, *Car to Dickebusch. Across lake to Ridgewood, Dead Dog Farm, P & O, Bois Carré, new reserve line, Crater Lane, Front Line to P & O. Home via Ringwood and Vierstraat Road. Bosch guns active, 4.2s and 5.9s on ridge behind Ridgewood and right battalion HQ as I was going up from the lake. Many on Brasserie Road. Some grenades and 'minnies' on head of Crater Lane. Shells being scattered all over back areas. Our G car got a direct hit near Café Belge and was wrecked. Luckily Cox (the driver) had just abandoned ship and hidden. That evening Claud dined at the club in Poperinghe.*[82]

The Toc H in Poperinghe. The chapel (below) as it is today – still under the eaves but no longer 'dim and dark'

© Tony Potter 2009

© Tony Potter 2009

A week later Claud arranged to do a week's tour in the trenches to experience the dreadful conditions in which the unfortunate infantry had to live. On a beautiful bright moonlit night the front was quiet. He visited the Bluff where considerable mining activity was taking place. After two days his visit was cut short as Plumer wanted to see the baths and camps and Claud was required to be present. The visit went well, despite heavy rain, and the *Army Commander got a bit muddy, I fear!*

Now that the Somme battle was over and restrictions on ammunition expenditure had been lifted, the artillery on both sides became more active, supplemented by the fearsome, clumsy but highly

[82] Poperinghe. The Ypres Museum Guide *In Flander's Fields*, p.22 describes the town as "the focal point of the British sector. Poperinghe's narrow streets were crammed with thousands of troops, pieces of artillery on heavy carriages, cyclists, ambulances, cavalry units and London buses bringing in fresh troops. You could buy the London newspapers and eggs and chips, go to a film or watch a live show. The officers liked to drink at La Poupe or in some of the other officer only eating houses." Toc H (Talbot House) which was open to all ranks, still exists "the dim, dark chapel under the eaves remains a deeply moving way-station to any pilgrim to the Western Front." Keegan, ibid p.200.

effective short range trench mortars directed against the trenches by both sides, the German version being the more effective compared with the British Stokes mortar. Long range guns were used to shell the rear areas. When one, probably a railway gun, dropped shells uncomfortably close to the divisional headquarters in Reninghelst, the laundry girls fled and refused to return unless their wages were increased. One afternoon whilst out riding, Claud heard a howitzer shell getting nearer and nearer. He realised it was coming pretty close and looked around for a nice soft place to fall in. The shell fell a hundred yards away. Luckily it was a dud. *It did not take Sandy long to do 200 yards to a flank and by the time the next ones came we were well out of the danger zone.*

By now there was a marked increase in air activity, as both sides wrestled for air superiority with improved, faster and more manoeuvrable aircraft, in particular the Sopwith Camel of the Royal Flying Corps and the German Fokker tri-plane in which the ace, Baron von Richthofen, destroyed 80 aircraft. Claud saw the tri-planes of Richthofen's air circus, painted red with white tails, fly low over the front line, to be beaten off by unusually accurate anti-aircraft fire. The German bombers carried out raids on towns in the rear areas, such as Poperinghe and Ballieul, which, with their shops and eating places, represented comparative civilisation for troops out of the line.

During the bitter winter weather, activities by both sides in the IX Corps and X Corps areas were largely confined to raids on the opposing trenches, some mounted by a handful of reluctant soldiers, others involving a battalion or even a brigade. They were unpopular with the soldiers who would have preferred to live and let live, but headquarters staff insisted that they were necessary to keep alive an offensive spirit on an otherwise static battlefield, to keep the enemy off balance and to obtain intelligence. However, the amount of valuable intelligence some miserable private soldier taken prisoner could provide seems unlikely to have been important enough to justify the cost of the raids in lives lost. According to Cyril Falls "the British raided too often." [83] Claud watched one of these raids on 24 February, mounted by 10th Queen's against the Hollandischaeloeum

---

[83] *The History of the 36th (Ulster) Division*, Cyril Falls.

Redoubt. *Zero hour at 4.55. Second line reached and much damage done. One officer and 54 other ranks taken prisoner. I saw the show from the old reserve line. Barrage magnificent and sudden. Appearance of the planes out of the mist most awfully well done. Hun hardly appeared to retaliate and was taken completely by surprise. Prisoners a poor looking lot, Saxons, and did not seem particularly upset at being taken. Our casualties at about 12 ORs killed and 105 wounded, mostly slightly.*

Claud escaped from all this in the last week of April for three weeks leave, the longest time he had been home since the halcyon pre-war summer of 1914. He attended the investiture at Buckingham Palace to receive his DSO and spent what must have been a blessed four days in Devonshire. When he returned to France, the long cold winter and spring were over. It was extremely hot, so much so that ironically there were concerns about a possible water shortage.

The coming of spring produced greatly increased activity. On the front there was an improvement of the trenches. In the rear, there was the arrival of reinforcements, the building of a vast new railhead at Bailleul, the laying of light railway lines, tramways and timber tracks to transport forward enormous quantities of artillery ammunition to the dumps, and in the case of the heavy artillery right to the gun positions. Ever mindful of security, Claud in his diaries gave no hint of these preparations for a spring offensive, apart from a brief reference to a visit to Vormezeele to make traffic and tramway arrangements.

It was left to the assistant priest of Dickebusch to give an account of the preparations as he observed them. "June 3rd 1917. Sunday. Incredible the number of soldiers now staying in Reninghelst. I would put their number at 45,000 and there are certainly 15,000 horses. At least 250 cars and lorries pass the church every hour. The streets are busier than the biggest streets in Brussels in peacetime. What good business the innkeepers and tradesmen are doing right now!" [84]

Haig had long been nurturing a plan to mount an offensive through Flanders south of Ypres with a view to breaking through to the

---

[84] *In Flander's Fields*, the guide to the museum in the old Cloth Hall in Ypres.

German railhead at Roulers and then pushing on to the coast where, supported by an amphibious landing, he hoped to capture the main U-boat bases at Ostend and Zeebrugge. In December the Germans had adopted a policy of unrestricted submarine warfare, including attacks on American ships, which resulted in an American declaration of war on 6 April 1917. A convoy system was introduced, but the U-boats continued to operate in coastal waters where individual ships were unescorted. There was growing concern that they might succeed in starving the civilian population in Britain.

However, Haig's idea had to be put on hold as Lloyd George, who had taken over as Prime Minister from Asquith in December 1916, had agreed that the British would support a spring offensive by the French south of the Somme. These plans had to be revised when unexpectedly the Germans straightened out their front and thereby saved twenty divisions by withdrawing to a new front line running from Bapaume to the Aisne. Known as the Hindenburg Line, it had been well prepared and was exceptionally strong with massed wire defences. The withdrawal was carried out by degrees between 25 February and 5 April 1917. In withdrawing they carried out widespread and wilful destruction in their wake, houses, farms, churches set on fire, their contents desecrated, woods and orchards felled, farm animals slaughtered or stolen. The Allies followed up slowly, for the ground was a sea of mud and speed was impossible.

The British opened their offensive on 9 April with an attack at Arras, whilst four Canadian divisions captured Vimy Ridge, one of the most successful operations of the whole war. However, in both instances the Allies failed to exploit these initial successes. The weather at Arras was atrocious, rain, sleet and snow and the daily average of British casualties was higher than it had been on the Somme. The attacks had been intended to distract German attention from the French offensive mounted a week later with an attack towards the Chemin des Dames. The results were another disaster. By the time Nivelle, who had succeeded Joffre as the Commander-in-Chief, called off the attack on 9 May, they had lost 100,000 men. The morale of the French army was broken and 50 divisions mutinied, refusing to undertake any further attacks. It was accepted that for the moment the British would have to fight on alone.

Haig was now in a position to push ahead with his plan to break through to the Channel ports by mounting the first phase of what was to become the Third Battle of Ypres – the capture of Messines Ridge. Although quite a modest feature, it was high enough to enable the enemy to overlook the British front and rear areas as far back as Mont Kemmel and Mont des Cats.

All through the winter and spring of 1917, the tunnelling companies had been constructing galleries leading to mine chambers under the German line from Hill 60 to Ploegstraat Wood, packed with a million tons of explosive.

The attack of 7 June was to be undertaken by nine divisions of the Second Army, including the Australians, New Zealanders, the 16th (Irish) and the 36th (Ulster) Divisions, veterans of the first day on the Somme, with Claud's division, the 41st Division, assaulting from its front line on either side of St Eloi. The artillery had amassed 2,266 guns, including 756 heavies, and 144,000 tons of ammunition, enough for a thousand rounds per gun for the 18 pounders. The Germans, realising that an attack was being planned, had massed over 200 batteries. The artillery duel began at the beginning of May and went on for a month, the rear areas increasingly coming under fire.

The final bombardment started on 21 May, increasing to maximum intensity on 31 May, with the RFC providing no fewer than 300 aircraft to direct the fire of the guns on strong points, trenches and enemy batteries. In *The Gunner* magazine 82 years later, a subaltern movingly described walking up to an OP on Mont Kemmel to watch the last hours of the bombardment and the detonation of the mines. The hill "looked delightfully pretty and refreshing with its covering of trees in the fresh green foliage." On their way they stopped at the base of the hill to watch a howitzer battery in action. "We remained a few minutes and then continued up the path, passing in due course a delightfully pretty cottage covered with green creeper and inhabited by a family of peasants. Just above the cottage we met the daughter of the house coming down the hill with her arms full of wild flowers, a fresh looking girl of about 18. The whole scene struck me as extraordinary, the bright sunshine of early June, the blue sky flecked with white clouds, the shady path enclosed by trees and bushes, the little cottage and the girl with the flowers, the occasional note of a bird, and there, at the base of the hill, the great guns with their straining crews, the loud detonations, the scream of the shells." According to the same writer the bombardment was distinctly heard on the Sussex Downs; in Folkestone and Dover windows rattled and shook with the concussion; and at night silent crowds collected on the cliffs and gazed anxiously across the Channel to where the whole horizon was lit up with a constant flickering glare.[85]

The infantry battle opened at 3.10 am with the battalions going over the top behind the intense barrage. Claud was watching from the roof of some dugouts less than a mile from the start line. He had an exciting drive out to the rendezvous in the car, with shells dropping over the road. Near Segard Château (I30) they encountered gas shells, several falling only a few yards away and they had to take cover in a deep muddy ditch. *I shall never forget seeing the St Eloi, Hill 60 and Messines mines going up*, he wrote. *The ground swayed under us like an earthquake, followed by huge sheets of red and yellow flame and columns of debris and black smoke. The barrage was a fine sight too. Too dark to see the infantry going over the top. Strolled into Vormezeele. Very little Hun retaliation.* Of the 24 mines, 19 had detonated. The shock rocked buildings within a 30 mile radius and a seismograph in Switzerland recorded a small earthquake.[86] The effect was devastating, the defenders who survived were numbed and unable to react. By evening all the objectives had been taken, including the villages of Messines and Wytschaete, the latter by 41st Division.

Casualties had been comparatively light considering the scale of the operation. The Germans lost 13,000 killed and wounded, and at least another 7,500 taken prisoner. *We can't make out what was wrong with Fritz,* Claud wrote the next day. *He put up no fight at all. What happened to his guns? MGs practically nil and gun barrage negligible.* He spent the day walking over the battlefield. *Hun lines fearfully knocked about and wire flattened except opposite the Mud*

[85] *Some Impressions of the Bombardment of Messines* by Lieutenant G H Thompson, published in *The Gunner*, October 2001. Press reports spoke of the explosion of the mines being heard in London. In fact according to Claud they made no sound at all, though the barrage was like hell let loose and could well have been heard across the Channel.

[86] Five mines did not explode. One of these exploded in 1955, probably set off by lightning. The other three are still in the ground and two are under occupied farm buildings.

Patch where the damage was not great. Hun dugouts made of huge concrete blocks, a wonderful sight and many quite undamaged despite our terrific bombardment. Place littered with mgs, TMs, bombs, rifles, equipment, etc. Hun position one of great natural strength overlooking the whole of our front and back areas. Can't think how he ever allowed us to move in our trenches. Mine crater at St Eloi is about 30 feet deep and nearly 100 yards across. Not many dead lying about. A good many on the Damstrasse, both ours and Bosch, and also in front of the craters. No shooting by the Huns, in fact things were most peaceful and troops and transport wandering about unconcerned everywhere.

It had been a famous victory, but it was followed by a great error which led directly to the Third Battle of Ypres. Instead of exploiting their success, the British waited a month. Lloyd George was worried about the mounting casualties, already a quarter of a million dead since 1914, and he had doubts about Haig's plan. In the end the Prime Minister agreed. By then there were only six days left before the offensive was due to begin and at that point the weather broke.

In the aftermath of Messines the German artillery was deliberately targeting Reninghelst with 8 inch long-range guns. *It was most exciting lying in bed and hearing 'slippery dick' coming along and wondering whether this was going to send you flying through the roof,* Claud told his mother. Although not much damage was done, some of the heavy shells came exceedingly close. Eventually the decision was taken to move the headquarters to a delightful nearby village, Westoutre. Claud's billet was in a lace shop with two most attractive women on the premises. *I am the envy of the division.* On 1 July the division moved back into a rest area centred on Berthen, with the headquarters in a small *château. Madame is very nice and there are 3 little girls, ages 10 to 16. Such nice children and the eldest flapper is very pretty. I am taking time to brush up my French.*

There was not much for Claud to do. He was heartily sick of staff work. He had heard that there was a shortage of senior gunner officers and he felt it was time for him to return to regimental duty. The divisional commander, General Lawford, wrote a glowing report to go with his application. His time with 41st Division was drawing to a close. Two weeks later he received terribly bad news.

Chapter 8   KEN

Kenneth, his younger brother, followed in Claud's footsteps, passing out from the Royal Military Academy at Woolwich and receiving his commission in the Royal Field Artillery in 1901. He served in the artillery barracks at Newbridge on the Curragh. As a skilled horseman he raced at Punchestown and was Master of the Kildare Hunt. By 1914 he had been posted to India and was living in one of the comfortable bungalows in Nowshera, 30 miles east of Peshawar on the North West Frontier. He took full advantage of all that the old India could offer. He hunted with the Peshawar Vale and went on *shikar*, shooting a bear in Kashmir and a tiger in the Central Provinces.

In 1915 the Mohmands in the tribal territory to the north were reported to be assembling to attack the British outposts. In August information was received that 10,000 tribesmen were moving down the Swat Valley to attack the fort at Chakdara. The Malakand Moveable Column was mobilised, consisting of four Indian Army battalions, a field and a mountain battery. Ken joined the column as staff officer to the artillery commander. The batteries engaged targets across the river, firing 335 rounds. For several nights the tribesmen sniped the camp from the surrounding hills with little success. For Ken it was his first experience of coming under fire. By October the tribesmen had called off their *jihad* and gone home, but not before the 21st Lancers in a cavalry charge at Shabkadar, further to the west, had lost their commanding officer and two officers, both friends of Ken.[87]

---

[87] For a few weeks I lived in one of the Nowshera bungalows. On New Year's Day 1947 a fellow subaltern and I borrowed a jeep and drove over the Malakand Pass to Chakdara, probably a foolish venture without an escort. I did not know then that I was following in my uncle's footsteps.

Ken (right) as
Master of the
Kildare Hunt

Ken had enjoyed the excitement, but it was a minor scrap compared with what was happening on the other side of the world. As he read in the growing casualty lists the names of men with whom he had served at Woolwich and in Ireland, he was impatient to become involved in the real war. However, for the moment it was the policy in India that only majors would be posted to units in action in Belgium and France. Although his promotion came through that November, it was another nine months before he arrived home. By November 1916 he was commanding the 4.5 howitzer battery in 52nd Army Field Artillery Brigade, deployed close to Arras, with passable accommodation in an old house half blown away, but with deep cellars. It was typical of him that he had made it as comfortable as possible for his men, *a nice kitchen, dining hall, bathroom, wash house and drying room*. On Christmas morning he challenged a Royal Horse Artillery battery as to which could fire the most rounds in half a minute. Word had gone round and a crowd of spectators turned out to watch. Ken's battery won. The prize, a bottle of port, went down well with the Christmas dinner of *pâté de fois gras*, soup, turkey, plum pudding and savoury.

By the time of the Battle of Arras in April 1917, the artillery had learned valuable lessons from the Somme battles of the previous year, including perfecting the creeping barrage. Shells were more reliable and had been armed with proximity fuses. The whole battlefield had been photographed from the air, at grievous cost to airmen's lives. Techniques in flash spotting and sound ranging had been developed, enabling the locations of enemy artillery to be passed back to batteries allocated for counter battery fire and for the guns to be corrected onto the target. Ken's battery, deployed at St Nicholas, a suburb on the north side of Arras, had been detailed for this role and had been allocated a wireless and a mast to receive corrections to their fire, although the sets had only limited range of about 7,000 yards and were heavy, taking four men to lift.

The bombardment began on 4 April. 2,879 guns, including 989 heavies, and over two and a half million shells had been assembled, the greatest mass of artillery the world had ever seen, co-ordinated in a way that had never before been achieved. 24,000 reserves had been moved into the safety of a huge underground network tunnelled out of the chalk below the streets of Arras, extending almost to the front line, enabling units to move unseen into battle positions.

Zero hour was 5.30 am on 9 April. Conditions were appalling: sleet and snow driven on a gale, the ground churned to ankle-deep mud, as the infantry tried, but did not always succeed, in keeping pace with the creeping barrage. Results on the first day were a triumph. The German front was penetrated to a depth of one to three miles, and 9,000 prisoners were taken. In a spectacular attack the four divisions of the Canadian Corps captured the commanding feature of Vimy Ridge, dominating the Douai Plain to the east.

52nd Brigade had been allocated to the 9th Division, supporting the South African Brigade. Twice Ken's brigade had had to hook in and deploy forward to keep pace with the infantry advance. In the bitter weather and heavy ground *the bombardment nearly killed us all*, Ken found time to write to his mother, *with heavy snow on the ground, it was no fun sleeping under a sheet of corrugated iron.*

Thereafter, the advance began to bog down. Many of the infantry had no previous experience of battle and were inadequately trained.

In the atrocious weather conditions the divisions became exhausted. The Germans brought up their reserves, including artillery, which made extensive use of gas. Ken had become a victim, swallowing some of the poison. For three or four days he felt very ill, but refused to be evacuated, for fear of losing command of his battery.

By 17 May the offensive had been called off. Apart from Vimy, it had achieved very little. Average daily losses had been over 4,000, more than on the Somme. Ken's brigade had suffered heavily. Arras was "an enormous artillery duel and in the duelling the British on the whole emerged the winners, but only just." [88]

On 26 May Ken's brigade was withdrawn from Arras and was sent northward to join 41st Division, Claud's division. The brigade had suffered heavy casualties. Ken was greatly relieved to get away. Claud was up early to meet the train at the railhead near Poperinghe. It was due at 5.30 am, but the town was being shelled and it was 7 pm before it arrived. Ken was amazed to find his brother waiting for him. He took him back to the divisional mess for a meal to celebrate their reunion. It was at least three years since they had met. It was a great relief to be able to talk brother to brother, exchanging memories of childhood, schooldays at Marlborough and the good life before the war. Ken brought news of home, their two sisters – both now married and one had had the first grandchild – as well as news of their widowed mother, who was suffering from depression. And there was the bond of shared suffering, horror and terror – the kind of talk that was not spoken in the presence of their women. In the previous six weeks at Arras, Ken had gone through a terrible time, suffered experiences he had never before known, yet *I've never seen him so fit*, Claud wrote. *We had by far the warmest and most affectionate meeting we have ever had.*

52nd Brigade was allocated little time to recover. Within five days it was deployed between Dickebusch and Voormazeele, leaving one gun per battery back in the wagon lines as a reserve. Ken's howitzers were at Gordons' Farm (N5a), just east of the lake. On the night of 31 June the causeway across the south west end of the lake came under heavy hostile fire, both high explosive and gas.

---

[88] Farndale, ibid p.182.

A water cart and an ammunition wagon were hit, blocking the way. There was pandemonium as men donned their gasmasks and struggled to put masks on the terrified horses. Ken saw what was happening from his battery position and went to help. He ordered the horses to be unhitched and taken back in the direction of Dickebusch and the causeway to be cleared. Finding he could not make himself heard while wearing his gas mask, he removed it to shout orders and, in doing so, he suffered severely from gas poisoning. Having succeeded in clearing the way, he collapsed. His actions had undoubtedly saved the lives of many men and horses. He was recommended for an immediate award of the Distinguished Service Order.

As soon as Claud heard the news he borrowed a car and went out to look for his brother. He had great difficulty in finding the battery position and brought him back through heavy shellfire. The causeway was littered with wagons and dead horses. Minutes after they had got across, 20 gas shells fell a few yards away. Although he was conscious and seemed cheerful, Ken was evacuated to a casualty clearing station and thence to 14 General Hospital at Boulogne. The War Office telegram said he had been severely gassed. By then it was policy that all gas casualty were sent home to recuperate, lest complications should develop. He was sent home for three weeks sick leave. He spent some time at a village inn, the 'Crook and Shears', at Upper Clatford,[89] fishing on the River Test. It was the best possible remedy, absolute peace. The old people who owned the place were very kind to him. He reckoned if he had stayed any longer there, he would soon have weighed 16 stone.

At the end of June Ken returned to his battery. Claud borrowed the general's car to fetch him from Boulogne. Both the division and the battery were out of the line at rest, the former at Berthen, the latter a mile away. The two brothers spent all the time they could in each other's company, walking through the old German lines and meeting several times for dinner. On 7 July Claud invited Ken and his CO, Belcher, to an evening at 'Crumps', the divisional concert party, followed by dinner.

---

[89] Still there in 2012.

Ken's grave at Dickebusch
in 1923 and 2009 and
(below) a copy of the
recommendation for DSO
for Major Ken Potter RFA

52nd Army FA	Brigade:	41st Division:	Xth Corps:	15/6/17	Date of Recommendation

Unit	Regtl No	Rank and Name	Action for which commended	Recommended by	Honour or Award
'D' Battery 52nd Brigade RFA		Major, Kenneth Mitchell POTTER RFA	On the night of May 31st and June 1st 1917, during the bombardment of WYSCHAETE RIDGE, a block in the traffic on the track across the S.W. end of DICKEBUSCH LAKE, occurred, owing to a water cart and an ammunition wagon being hit by a shell. The track was being heavily shelled with gas shells. Major POTTER, whose battery was close to the lake, went amongst the transport to restore order, and clear the track. Finding he could not make himself understood with his respirator on, he removed the latter to shout orders, and in doing so suffered severely from gas. After clearing the traffic, he completely collapsed from the effect of the gas. His action undoubtedly, was the means of saving lives of many men and horses. RECOMMENDED FOR IMMEDIATE AWARD. *Sidney Lawford* Major General Commanding 41st Division June 18th 1917	Lieut Col H.T. Belcher, DSO Commanding 52nd Army F.A. Brigade	DSO

Two days later in the early hours Claud was woken by an orderly, bringing tragic news. Ken was dead. Heartbroken, he dressed and went for a walk alone round Mont des Cats. At daybreak he went to the battery to obtain the details. The brigade recce party, including Belcher, the brigade commander, Ken and one of the subalterns had gone forward to look for new gun positions north of the Comines canal. Somewhere between Chester Farm (I33a) and The Bluff (I34c) all three had been killed by the same shell. Later that day confirmation came through that Ken had been awarded a DSO. The citation had been signed by Belcher. It was policy that immediate awards should be given priority, lest the recipient should be dead before he knew. Ken never knew. [90]

The three officers lie side-by-side in Dickebusch cemetery, just across the fields from the causeway where Ken won his DSO. One of his fellow battery commanders wrote "we were all together just before the shell came. I'm going to the funeral this afternoon. The place is rich in colour with poppies, thistles and forget-me-nots." He went on "He is the godfather of my little son and was one of the most wonderful men I have ever met. An oculist of great power and a man of rare gifts in the art of making others happy. He made D/52 the happiest mess I have ever seen or served in." There were many such letters. "There will be great grief in the battery, for every officer, NCO and man had the greatest love and respect for him. There is not one of us who would not have thought it an honour to die for him. A straighter man and a finer English gentleman it would be hard to find." Another letter read, "He was a most extraordinarily popular man, known and liked by everyone, generals, big people, *et al.* He will always remain for me the personification of keenness, energy and devotion to duty." He was indeed a much loved man.

The two brothers had found a love they had not realised until those last weeks. Claud wrote to their mother *the meeting out here has made such a different sort of affection. War has a great effect on one's feelings. A very deep love had sprung up between us. Let your pride in his glorious death – a death that every soldier, and Ken in particular, would choose – help you to bear your grief.*

---

[90] He was awarded a posthumous Mention-in-Despatches in November 1917

Chapter 9   PASSCHENDAELE
22 July – 23 August 1917

On 22 July Claud returned to France, leaving his mother in Ilkley, where she could draw some comfort from being amongst the friends from the years of her marriage. The family house, Arundel Lodge, had been sold and she was staying for a fortnight in the Royal Hotel. For Claud it had been a bittersweet interlude. The weather had been glorious. He had never seen the moors and the English countryside looking more beautiful, nor the Channel bluer. He had spent the last night in London with the Elliot Coopers [91] before boarding the leave boat at Folkestone. A staff car was waiting for him at Boulogne to take him back to 41st Division headquarters, still at Berthen. It had been an uneventful journey apart from two punctures, not surprising considering the state of the roads and that there were six passengers in the car. During the night enemy aircraft flew low over the headquarters area, one directly over Claud's billet. The night was rent with the sounds of machine guns and anti-aircraft guns. The sky was criss-crossed

---

[91] The Elliott Coopers were family friends, originally from Leeds. Sir Robert was a contemporary of Claud's father at Leeds Grammar School and for several years was resident engineer on a railway under construction in Yorkshire. He carried out many other railway and engineering works in Britain and overseas, including Nigeria. During the war he was chairman of the War Office Committee of the Council of Civil Engineers. He died in 1942, aged 97. He was the grandson of Captain John Elliott who had accompanied Captain Cook on his second and third voyages. His younger son, Neville, served in the Royal Fusiliers, was awarded a DSO and MC, and died in a German prisoner of war camp from wounds received in an action on 30 November 1917, for which he was awarded the Victoria Cross.

with searchlight beams, but the bombs that were dropped were nowhere near the headquarters.

Claud found that the division was deployed along the Ypres-Comines canal on the south side of the salient, with two of the infantry brigade headquarters in the tunnels built into Spoil Bank (I33a). Until a vacancy occurred for command of an artillery brigade, Claud was attached to the division's 187th Artillery Brigade, which had its headquarters at Dead Dog Farm (N6b).

The Third Battle of Ypres, or Passchendaele began in mid June 1917 with a preliminary bombardment. By mid July the greatest concentration of artillery ever seen up to that time had been deployed in and around the salient, 2,866 guns of all calibres. The 18 pounders were so packed in the confined space that in some places they were almost wheel to wheel. The Germans had deployed with fewer numbers, 1,556 guns. However, they had two vital advantages: the high ground of Pilckem Ridge in the north; and the Gheluvelt Plateau straddling the Menin Road in the south. Elsewhere the slight ridges rising from the streams enabled them to overlook most of the battlefield, whilst keeping their batteries out of sight on the reverse slopes. The British had to rely largely on observation balloons and the Royal Flying Corps to provide observation of fire. Many times Claud mentions aerial battles as the two sides fought for air supremacy.

For the British gunners, conditions in the batteries were appalling. There was no hope of concealing their positions. Camouflage was well nigh impossible, since there was nothing with which to camouflage the guns, apart from a sheet of corrugated iron laid over a shell hole. Once deployed it required many men and horses to move a gun into a new position. They were constantly in action, constantly under fire. In the course of the preliminary bombardment alone, the guns had fired nearly three million shells. Frequently they had to don their gas masks, as the Germans made extensive use of gas shells, including for the first time mustard gas. They suffered heavy casualties. "The conditions in which they eked out their miserable existence simply made matters worse as their physical and mental health began to give way under the strain." [92]

---

[92] *Passchendaele, The Sacrificial Ground,* Nigel Steel and Peter Hart, p.187.

"Many detachments had almost no rest or relief and were at near exhaustion at a time when they should have been most alert." [93]

Dead Dog Farm was in the midst of a concentration of heavy artillery. *One of the 9.2s was practically in our mess and nearly knocked you down when it fired.* Claud had moved into a dugout close by, opposite Elzenwalle Château (H36b), where Ken's CO had had his headquarters. When the farm came under accurate shell fire and one shell had landed three yards from the mess, the brigade headquarters joined him in the dugout.

Claud passed the time visiting the batteries and the infantry brigade headquarters in Spoil Bank. The whole area was within range of the German bombardment. At one of the batteries Claud had several more narrow escapes. One night there was a gas attack. *It was pretty strong and we had to put on respirators. Made one sneeze terribly, in fact gave one a severe cold in the head.* Twice Claud tried to visit Ken's old battery, but each time he had to turn back because of the intensity of the shell fire. The battery had suffered very heavily since Ken's death, with 30 casualties, including his groom.

Two nights before Zero Day, Claud went beagling in the old reserve line with a pack consisting of *a terrier of sorts and 2 lurchers provided by the detachment of a neighbouring 6 inch battery. We got two rabbits but missed a fine hare.*

By the end of July the Allied armies were in position and ready for the assault, First French Army in the north, Gough's Fifth Army, the main force, in the centre and Plumer's Second Army in the south. Their aim was to take and hold the dominating ground of Pilckem Ridge and Gheluvelt Plâteau. At 3.50 am on 31 July the divisions advanced under the mightiest creeping barrage that had ever been witnessed up to that time. Despite the fact that the weeks of bombardment had destroyed the drainage system, causing extensive flooding, the attack on the northern flank went well. The French had made significant advances and Pilckem Ridge was in British hands. However, the attacks in the south had come to a halt without gaining the plâteau.

---

[93] Farndale, ibid p.204

108

The Germans had developed a new form of defence – no longer a trench system but lines of concrete pillboxes, unconnected but with interlocking arcs of fire, and containing machine guns. The forward areas were lightly held, with the main force well back, out of range of field artillery and immediately ready to mount a counter attack.

At 2 pm the Germans mounted such a counter attack against the centre division, supported by low flying aircraft armed with bombs and machine guns, possibly the first time that aircraft had been used in close support of ground forces. The British divisions which, in many cases, had lost contact with their supporting artillery, with telephone lines cut and drizzling rain making observation impossible, were driven back to their start line running south from St Julien (C12c). By evening the weather had broken with a vengeance, the drizzle had become a downpour. One of the centre divisions, 55th Division, had suffered so greatly, reduced in numbers and in a state of fatigue, that the corps commander ordered that the battalions must be relieved forthwith by 36th (Ulster) Division.

After taking part in the battle for Messines Ridge in June, the Ulstermen had been withdrawn to a rest area south west of St Omer, leaving their divisional artillery still deployed to contribute to the bombardment in support of 55th Division. For the battalions the time spent in the rest area was almost idyllic. The nights were warm enough to sleep out or in tents pitched in the cherry orchards. There was good trout fishing in the streams. The 12 days of rest and training ended with a gymkhana. Then at the end of July the battalions moved in long convoys of buses and lorries to the rear area of XIX Corps between Watou and Poperinghe. At 4 am on 4 August the divisional headquarters took over from 55th Division, with the artillery and infantry brigade headquarters in the deep mine workings at Wieltje (C28b). The entrance to the tunnels regularly came under shellfire and it was there on 3 August that the commanding officer of 153rd Brigade, Lieutenant Colonel Roger Thompson, was wounded. Claud was chosen to take over the Brigade.[94]

---

[94] It is interesting to reflect that the chance shell was the first link in the chain that led to our family making its home in Northern Ireland.

On Zero Day 31 July, Claud had watched from a lookout beside his dugout, 41st Division go into battle on either side of the canal, about 2½ miles away. The division, a formation in Second Army, was the link between the two armies in their attack to take Gheluvelt Plâteau. On the left 123rd Brigade advanced out of Battle Wood (H35d) to attack the trenches on the Klein Zillebeke road. *The going was very heavy, water filled shell holes, slippery craters, slimy mud.* Next day Claud called at 122nd Brigade headquarters in Spoil Bank to find out how the day had gone. *Our part of the show did not go well. Zero Hour too early and our troops lost direction. II Corps (the right hand Corps of the Fifth Army) on the Hooge-Battle Wood front met much opposition and did not progress at all well. Prisoners now 5,000, but no guns. Not much for an attack by a whole Army and four Corps.*

On two more occasions Claud had tried to visit Ken's old battery on the other side of the canal. It was not just a desire to commiserate with his brother's soldiers on their heavy losses, he needed to learn something about the problems of deploying the howitzers, since one of the batteries in his brigade would be equipped with these heavier guns. Both times he had to turn back as shells were falling, first on the canal crossing, then on Spoil Bank (I33a). He had several narrow shaves. *As we got to Spoil Bank 8 inch shells began arriving. One fell on the bank beside us, another pitched where we had passed only a few minutes after we got into the tunnel.*

The weather features prominently in the diary. *1 August, perfectly filthy day. Commencing yesterday evening poured incessantly for 24 hours. Ground a regular sponge and mud unmentionable. Presume it will interfere very much with our operations. 2 August, filthy day again, rain nearly whole day. State of ground too indescribably beastly. Walked over in evening to see 9.2 gun on railway line behind English Copse. Found it badly sunk in the mud. Looks as if this present weather might last for weeks. Fear our autumn offensive has opened with all the luck against us. 3 August, poured rain without ceasing. State of ground defies description.*

According to a lieutenant colonel of the meteorological section at GHQ, "the rainfall directly affecting the first month of the offensive was more than double the average; it was over five times the amount for the same period in 1915 and 1916." [95] Haig could not say he had not been warned. His meteorological advisers had told him that he could not hope for more than a fortnight or at best three weeks of fine weather. [96]

On 3 August Claud called at the headquarters at Westoutre to say goodbye to the divisional staff who had been his fellow officers for the past ten months. He spent a last comfortable night in a billet in the village. Next day he called at the artillery headquarters in Abele to be told that his new brigade was still in support of 55th Division. He went on to XIX Corps where he met the BGRA, Brigadier General W B R Sandys, and then on by car to the divisional headquarters where he would have been told that since yesterday 153rd Brigade had reverted to being under command of 36th (Ulster) Division, its own division. He drove on through Ypres to St Jean and walked the rest of the way to his new brigade's headquarters, one of three in Wieltje mine (C28a). On the way he encountered strong gas and had to don his respirator.

Falls gives a vivid description of Wieltje mine. "None who saw it will forget that abominable mine with its 'town major', its thirteen entrances, the water that flowed down its narrow passages and damp pouring down its walls, the electric light gleaming dully through steam coated lamps, its sickly atmosphere, its smells, its huge population of men and rats. From behind sack-curtained doorways the coughing and groaning of men in uneasy slumbers mingled with the click of typewriters. In a corridor one would fall over a runner, slimy from head to foot with mud, resting whilst he waited for a return message to the front line. One advantage it had, it was safe. And that was in part counterbalanced by the entrances and exits constantly menaced by storms of fire." [97] In a letter to his mother Claud told her *there appears to be no ventilation. Four of us are living in a little alcove about 5ft x 5ft x 12ft. There we have to eat, sleep and do all our office work. For real discomfort it beats anything I have had to face in this war. All the roof and walls leak and the passages are several inches in water. The state of filth and smells are too awful.* In his diary he describes his headquarters as *at the bottom of*

---

[95] Passchendaele, ibid p.141.

[96] Liddell Hart, ibid p.427.

[97] Falls, ibid p.112.

a mine shaft 2,000 yards from Fritz who continually crumps the top,
though it is safe enough below. The atmosphere is almost unbearable.

In all circumstances, in peace and war, it is difficult to be accepted
by a closely knit group bound together by shared experiences that
the newcomer has not known. In the heat of battle it must have been
very difficult to assume command of soldiers who had been constantly
in action since coming under command of 55th Division on 7 July,
who were nearly at the end of their tether, and who would have been
understandably wary of an unfamiliar lieutenant colonel who had
spent the past two years in the relative safety of the staff. It is greatly
to Claud's credit (but no surprise to us who loved him) that he won
over the officers and men of his brigade from the outset.

On the evening of his arrival Claud visited his batteries, deployed
750 yards north east of Wieltje. They were in exposed positions,
constantly under shell fire and under observation from two enemy
aircraft that flew low overhead. The following day he moved them
back to less exposed positions round the ruins of St Jean. As they
struggled to move the guns through the mud, they came under heavy
shell fire and lost 20 men.

On 6 August Claud was designated Left Group commander with a
total of 12 batteries under command, including four each from 306th
and 307th Brigades of 61st Division, the former deployed along
Admiral's Road (C22) and the latter round St Jean, a total of 72 guns.
For someone who had just taken over command of a brigade for the
first time, it was a heavy responsibility, especially as he had been
suffering from a fever for four days. The assault towards Langemarck,
the next phase of Third Ypres, was due to be launched ten days
hence. There was so much to be done in so little time. It was difficult
to co-ordinate the fire of so many guns, draw up a fire plan and
deliver it to the batteries, probably by runner since the telephones
were frequently cut and there were as yet no wirelesses. In the hours
before the assault on Pilckem Ridge, a battery commander described
the difficulties. "It would be simple enough if one had a room with
a table and a good light to work with, but here in a mud hole with a
guttering candle it is very difficult indeed." [98]

---

[98] Farndale, ibid p.201.

New gun positions had to be selected further forward, initially round Wieltje, in a thunderstorm and later just behind the front line, to give maximum range cover for the infantry. The guns had to be moved in appalling conditions over thick, oozing mud, round shell holes practically touching. Anyone who fell in died a most terrible death, dragged down amongst old and new corpses and lingering gas. Horses, even guns, disappeared. Ammunition had to be carried forward by hand along paths made from railway sleepers and duckboards. Many mules and artillery horses died. All the while the German artillery kept up its bombardment with high explosives, shrapnel and gas. Night after night their bombers carried out air raids on the tented camps in the rear areas where 36th Division awaited orders to take up battle positions. Casualties in Claud's Left Group were heavy. D Battery of 153rd Brigade, the howitzer battery, was in the process of moving into new positions when six 5.9s fell amongst them. One of the officers, Captain Hardbord,[99] was killed and two other officers badly wounded. At one stroke Claud had lost *what were probably my three best officers.* That night in a battery of 307th Brigade the battery commander was wounded, a subaltern killed and 23 other ranks killed or wounded.

By now the observation posts were in position on the front line along Call Reserve, a lane running from NW to SE (C23c). Claud visited them several times to watch the practice barrage and to scan the area for uncut wire. He had several narrow escapes as the line came under fire, but by then the ground was so soft that shells tended to dig in well before exploding, limiting their lethal effect. On 11 August he was up before dawn to look for new positions just behind the front to cover the assault on Langemarck. *Evidently the road* [from Wieltje to Gravenstafel] *had had a very bad time just previously, as it was liberally peppered. Many dead lying about, evidently just killed.* The divisional pioneers and sappers had been given the task of keeping the roads clear and sustained heavy casualties. One sapper company lost three of its six officers killed and two wounded.

Later that day Claud walked back to Ypres where a car picked him up to take him to the divisional headquarters at Mersey Camp,

---

[99] Captain Stephen Hardbord MC was the 27 year old son of the Reverend Harry Hardbord of Colwood Park, Bolney, Sussex. He is buried in Vlamertinghe cemetery. Grave VI.E.7

mid-way between Poperinghe and Vlamertinghe for a final conference with General Sandys and Brigadier General Brock, the CRA, who provided tea.

Zero Hour for the battle for Langemarck was at 4.45 am on 16 August, postponed for two days because of the weather. IV Corps of Fifth Army took part, with XIX Corps in the centre, consisting of 36th (Ulster) Division on the left and 16th (Irish) Division on the right, their objective the ridge running from Zonnebeke towards St Julien. The day went reasonably well in the north with the capture of Langemarck, the village a heap of rubble, and St Julien. For the two Irish divisions the battle was a disaster. The battalions were at barely half their strength. Since taking over from 55th Division, the companies had come under heavy bombardment, shells, gas and air raids. Night after night battalions in tents were under aerial attack. Those already in the line had lost heavily, particularly in the final 24 hours as they waited in the trenches. Companies were reduced to an average of 70 men each. As a result fewer than 2,000 infantry went over the top. The forward wave consisted of fewer than 300 men, and their numbers were probably reduced by about a third in the first half minute.

As feared there had not been enough time to draw up a thorough fire plan. On the desolate wasteland of the battlefield, with all landmarks obliterated, it was very difficult to identify and register all the pillboxes. Some were not engaged at all in the bombardment. The pace of the barrage, a hundred yards in five minutes, proved to be far too fast. The companies, diverted to attack the pill boxes whence the machine guns were keeping up a withering fire, were unable to keep pace. "In these circumstances the Irish had little chance of success, and they made a pitiably weak sight as their lines straggled forward, lashed by machine gun bullets and scything fragments of shell. Groups of the most determined did manage to make small gains but for the most part their sacrifices were entirely in vain as the German counter attacks easily flung the two divisions back to their start line." [100] "Throughout the whole war this was the only attack by the 36th Division which suffered complete reverse", according to Falls. [101]

---

[100]   Steel and Hart, ibid p.148.

[101]   Falls, ibid p.120.

The battle was not a success from the artillery point of view. The tactics of the day demanded a thorough fire plan. It was essential to have time to prepare it, and this was not given. The result was that many of the key points in the bombardment were not dealt with. Then during the battle, because of the intense smoke, the infantry's SOS signals could not be seen, and the bombardment of every counter attack failed or was late. No attempt was made to use gas against the pill boxes. Surprisingly too, although the weather and air situation were good, only one spotter aircraft was in the air.[102] With all this Claud agreed. *I think our heavy artillery preparation was insufficient and the concrete dugouts containing machin-guns were not done in.* He watched the progress of the attack. *Barrage came down beautifully at zero hour. Hun retaliation was very rapid but not particularly heavy. I saw our fellows get Hill 35, apparently going strong under our barrage. An hour later saw them come streaming back from 'Somme' and 'Gallipoli', the Hun reoccupying the hill at under 3,000 yards range, the whole thing very plain through glasses. In afternoon observation very good and could see Hun moving about everywhere. In morning saw their reinforcements marching down from Passchendaele Ridge and along Hill 35 from Zonnebecke direction. Infantry lost very heavily, probably 50 – 60%* [out of battalions low in strength when they started]*, nearly all from mgs. Back areas little straffed and we got off very lightly. Total of six wounded only. Our aeroplanes did well but several brought down. A bad day, I fear.* In the last two days he had only four hours sleep.

That night, 18 August, 61st Division began the relief of the Ulstermen. The battalions were to have four days desperately needed but all too short rest before entraining to travel south to the next battle, Cambrai. The artillery remained deployed for a further week. Claud spent much of that time visiting the batteries of the Left Group and up at the Call Reserve OP, accompanied by Brock, the CRA. *The German artillery got on to us as we came over the ridge and we had to scurry like rabbits. Even the General ran! Saw a lot of Huns moving about. Several small HE round about us as we were leaving and again we ran. Saw one of our 'planes brought down in flames over St Julien. At first it seemed quite steady though burning fiercely. I fancy the poor fellows were burnt to death before the 'plane crashed. Saw one of them*

---

[102] Farndale, ibid p.204.

jump or fall out. Hun 'planes were very active over us. Lots of our fighters up but they don't seem to care to tackle the Bosch.

A sudden welcome but temporary break in the weather brought fine, hot days and seemed to result in increased aerial activity. *21 August, saw three 'planes go down over Passchendaele Ridge. 22 August, saw a grand aeroplane fight in the morning just overhead and very low down. A German pilot took on three of ours. I was quite glad he got away as he was a real plucky little beggar. Some of his 'plane was shot away but he got home ok. Some of the bullets landed in our trench.*

On 21 August the batteries were very heavily shelled, an area shoot with a large concentration of guns, their fire directed by an observation aeroplane. B Battery had four guns knocked out but the casualties were light, one dead and four wounded. When Claud visited the wagon lines, the brigade headquarters camp was under fire but, though shells fell amongst the men and horses, there were no casualties. The divisional ammunition column had not been so fortunate the previous night, losing over a 100 animals from bombs and shellfire.

On 22 August the 61st Division launched a successful local attack, regaining the Green Line from 'Winnipeg' to the top of Hill 35. Claud watched the barrage. *First saw barrage then infantry crawling up (towards Pond Farm) and finally the surrender of some thirty Huns. Heavy barrage on our trench when we were up there on Call Reserve and we just got into our dugout in time. Chased home by 5.9s, 4.2s and some black air bursts, some very close.* A German counter attack assembling behind Hill 35 that evening was broken up by the artillery before it could get underway.

It was Claud's last day at Passchendaele. Next afternoon he handed over command of the Left Group to 55th Division. He walked to Preston Dump, then rode for 17 miles by way of Vlamertinghe along what is now the N308, through Poperinghe, and finally to the rest area at Watou. *It was such a long time since I have been on a horse that my tail got quite sore*, he told his mother. *We are now out of the line for a few days rest, after which we are trekking off many miles from here. I must say I am glad to get the Brigade away from our last place. The batteries have had a pretty rotten time and are quite ready for a change of scene. We go off to our new place by train. I only wish we were going to march but I suppose at the present juncture they cannot afford to keep divisions on the road when every man is wanted in the front line.* The stark truth was that the British were running out of manpower. Men who had attempted to enlist in the heady days of 1914, but had been turned down on medical grounds, were now being conscripted to fill the gaps in the ranks.

The Gheluvet Plâteau which had dominated the battlefield from the start was finally overrun with the capture of Polygon Wood on 26 September and Broodseinde, north east of Zonnebeke on 1 October. At that point "even the most enthusiastic technical historians of the Great War concede that Haig should have called off the offensive."[103] But the battle went on despite the fact that only the ANZAC and Canadian Corps were fresh enough and able to continue the fight. It was the Canadians who, on 10 November, captured the heap of rubble that had been the village of Passchendaele and the Third Battle of Ypres was brought to an end.

There are still several versions but no certain figure of the total number of British and Commonwealth casualties during the battle. Holmes quotes 275,000 dead and wounded. Nearly 12,000 lie in Tyne Cot cemetery, the largest of the Commonwealth war cemeteries in the salient. Many of the headstones bear the anonymous inscription 'Known Unto God'. A memorial to the missing records the names of 34,957 from mid August 1917 until the end of the war. Many were swallowed up for ever in the mud. Three German pillboxes still stand within the cemetery. The Cross of Sacrifice stands on one of them.

The last survivor of the battle and the last soldier to have fought in the Great War, Harry Patch, died on 25 July 2009, aged 111.

---

[103] Keegan, ibid p.392

Chapter 10 THE BATTLE OF CAMBRAI
23 August – 31 December 1917

For the first time since Claud set sail for France with 24th Division in August, a gap now occurs in his diary. [104] From 6 October 1917 the entries are restricted to comments on the filthy weather, and from mid November cease altogether, apart from the account of the capture of the German Albatross fighter and the graphic description of the opening of the German counter offensive on the 30 November. Most of the information about the activities of the batteries during the battle and thereafter, until the diary begins again on 6 February 1918, is taken from the 153rd Artillery Brigade war diary, held in the National Archives at Kew.

Initially the new tank units had been grouped under the coded name of the 'Heavy Machine Gun Corps', until 27 July 1917, when the Tank Corps was formed. So far the tanks had been employed in three battles: on the Somme in September 1916; at Arras; and at Third Ypres. Although they had played a major role in the capture of Flers in the first instance, they had achieved little so far. Instead of being committed *en masse,* they had been deployed in penny packets over ground unsuitable for tank warfare, cut up by preliminary bombardment,

---

[104] Claud did begin keeping up the diary again for a week from 10–17 December, written on separate sheets of notepaper. In the last entry of 1917 he writes that there is a chance of a month's leave from 22 December. The leave came through, because the next volume begins on 6 February as he is leaving home to return to the front.

118

so that the machines soon became clogged with mud, stuck in shell craters or brought to a halt trying to cross trenches. Arguably they were used too soon, alerting the Germans to their existence before sufficient numbers had come off the production line to mount a concerted assault.

On 4 August, as the first phase of Third Ypres, the battle of Pilckem Ridge, floundered in the mud of Passchendaele, the commander of the Tank Corps, Brigadier General Elles, submitted a plan to commander Third Army for a mass tank attack over ground suitable for their deployment, the chalk downs west and south west of Cambrai, achieving surprise and ensuring that the ground had not been broken up by shell fire by dispensing with a preliminary prolonged barrage.

At much the same time, Brigadier General Tudor, CRA of 9th (Scottish) Division, had also drawn up a plan whereby the artillery could dispense with the preliminary target registration required for planning a barrage which, in the past, had alerted the enemy that an attack was imminent. To achieve this, every gun, the 18-pounders of the field brigades, the howitzers, the heavy 9.2s and railway guns, had to be surveyed in, so that all were on the same grid, an enormous task carried out by the Royal Engineers field survey companies. Every gun had to be calibrated by firing on ranges in the rear area to allow for the differences in muzzle velocity which would affect their ranges. Each battery was equipped with an artillery board on which the location of the gun position and the range and bearing to targets could be plotted.[105] Sound ranging techniques had been developed that enabled the location of enemy guns to be fixed with 90 per cent accuracy. Aerial photographs were available at 24 hours' notice.

The area chosen for the attack lay between the partially completed Canal du Nord in the west and the Canal de l'Escaut in the east. It was a quiet sector. It had not been fought over since the early days of the war, although the country to the west and on either side of the Canal du Nord had been laid waste by the Germans during their withdrawal to the Hindenburg Line. At the northern end of the proposed front, the line ran along the canal before turning

[105] They continued to be used by the batteries in the Second World War.

westwards. It was immensely strong, two formidable lines from 500 to 1,000 yards apart, consisting of deep, wide trenches, elaborate dugouts, in part built by Russian prisoners of war, and wire defences in three or four belts each at least 20 feet apart. Since the area had been so quiet, the Germans had had time and peace to develop the defence works. Yet for all its strength, that sector of the Hindenburg Line was held by only two divisions, one of which was a second rate Landwehr division.

The Third Army plan was to overrun the area between the two canals and drive northwards to seize the Bourlon Ridge, enabling the cavalry to break out and exploit to the Sensée river. If this was successful the German defences west of the Canal du Nord would be outflanked by ten miles and forced to withdraw. The initial assault would be carried out by five divisions and two tank brigades, a total of 350 tanks, supported by 1,003 guns of all calibres. The cavalry corps would be ready to exploit the breakthrough. The tanks would operate in groups of three, each carrying a fascine, a bundle of brushwood which, when dropped into a trench, would enable the machines to cross over. They would break passages through the wire, creating gaps for the infantry who would be following on immediately behind, ready to occupy the ground and eliminate any remaining pockets of resistance. There would be no preliminary barrage over the preceding days. Initially Haig's chief of staff had reservations. As a result Haig was slow to approve the plan and final approval was not given until 13 October.

From 23 to 28 August, following their withdrawal from the Passchendaele battle, the batteries of 153rd Brigade rested and licked their wounds in the rear area round Watou and St Laurens. For six weeks they had endured "battle conditions in their worst form, a huge expenditure of ammunition, heavy and continuous hostile counter battery fire, shelling of wagon lines, the scantiest of accommodation, mud and indescribable wretchedness." [106] D Battery, the howitzer battery in particular, was in a bad state.

On 28 August the brigade entrained at Bavinchove, the station for Cassel, travelling overnight to Bapaume, unaware that they were to

---

[106] Falls, ibid p.130

be the forerunners for a new battle on a new front. On arrival the brigades of 36th (Ulster) Division took over from 9th (Scottish) Division a long frontage of some 6,000 yards, for the most part to the east of the Canal du Nord. Claud took over as his brigade headquarters a small cottage in the village of Metz-en-Couture. *Mirabile dictum it still had a roof (there can't be a dozen such within the adjoining 100 square miles).*

On 1 September Claud wrote to his mother describing the countryside and thereafter kept her informed of their efforts to turn the cottage into a comfortable home. From the detraining station at Bapaume, he had ridden to the brigade holding area at Le Mesnil through country that a year ago, when he was on the Somme front, had been enemy territory.

We are now well into the recaptured territory. It is for all the world like Salisbury Plain. With rolling downs and absolutely no fences of any sort. Nestling in the hollows one sees little woods, each containing what was once a smiling and prosperous agricultural village. They are now one and all completely destroyed, not a house or cottage being left standing. It makes one mad to see it. It is pure wanton destruction, as to destroy the cottages and small brick houses can have no military value whatsoever. I would just like to bring a party of pacifists round these parts for a tour to show them what the brother German is really like. In spite of all the damage the country is still very pretty and, except for the villages, there is little sign of war to be seen – a few shell holes now overgrown and, of course, barbed wire everywhere. The land has probably been one year uncultivated and there are still excellent clover and lucerne crops all over the country, so our horses are having the time of their lives. The great feature of these parts is that it is absolutely quiet. You would hardly know there was a war on at all. I was up in the line yesterday for most of the day and only heard about half a dozen guns (ours) fired the whole time. After the doing we had in our last place, the peace and quiet are very welcome. I don't mind if we stay the winter here.

In later letters Claud described the progress in making the headquarters cottage comfortable, installing fireplaces and repairing the roof, doors and windows. In the ruined village there was no shortage of wood for repairs. The adjutant, who was home on leave,

had been detailed to bring back wallpaper and a hunting frieze. By 12 **121**
October the fine weather of the previous fortnight had broken, with
pouring rain, and strong south east winds, but the cottage was now
very comfortable, a lovely open grate in the mess. *We have put glass
in the windows and are now going to paint the walls and door.* A week
later he wrote that the beams in the roof had been repainted and
the walls washed with distemper. He now had a small hut of his
own, *lined with match boarding and painted a dark green and white.
My servant is very clever at that sort of thing, in fact he is most useful
all round, as in addition to being a carpenter he is a skilled painter,
bricklayer and haircutter.*

On taking over from the 9th Division, 153rd Brigade was deployed
in and around Haverincourt Wood. A Battery was forward, close to
the canal, B and D in the wood itself, C just outside Metz, whilst
the headquarters, comfortably set up in the cottage, shared the
wood and village with 107th and 109th Infantry Brigades. HQ 36th
Division was in Ytres. Although the Germans had felled many trees
to use in the building of the Hindenburg Line and left many more
lying on the ground, the wood still provided excellent cover from
view, a vital factor in ensuring that the Germans remained unaware
of the coming attack. The blackberries were particularly good too,
according to Claud!

Using the sketch map in Claud's diary, it was possible in 2009 to
find traces of the brigade layout. The row of houses that contained
the brigade headquarters and the cottage containing the mess
and Sandy's stable, rebuilt in the original fashion, still look out to
Havrincourt Wood. The farm track runs across the flat fields where
cattle graze. Partridges take flight, a deer runs into the wood. At the
entrance deep wheel tracks have been filled in with the rubble of
broken houses. On the right heaps of earth and craters mark where
the howitzer battery was deployed. On the left another spoil heap
covers the 109th Brigade dugout. A shaft, too dangerous to enter,
burrows down beneath the forest floor.

All through a blessedly fine September, an almost peacetime
existence developed behind the lightly held front line. Nissen huts
were erected, since there were no houses or barns left standing after
the German withdrawal. Competitions were held for the best kept

Claud's sketch map showing the locations of Headquarters 107th, 109th and 153rd Brigades prior to Cambrai.

Author at the entrance to HQ 109th Brigade (left) and at the site of the howitzer battery gun position in Havincourt Wood in 2009 (below)

billets. Day trips by lorry and train to Amiens were organised. Canteen stocks were fully replenished to make up for the absence of shops. Beer was provided in large quantities to replace the supplies from the lost *estaminets*.

The divisional artillery column held a steeplechase. Claud rode in the first race and was going well until his horse was crossed at the water jump and ran out. He met many friends, including 'Tim' Pile who after the war was to become his adjutant in Cologne.[107]

Not all life was peaceful, however. At the front line the defences were improved, elaborate new dugouts excavated, ammunition dumps established. Raids were carried out against lightly held enemy outposts, mainly on a relatively small scale. The artillery was kept busy, having an ample supply of 18-pounder ammunition. Corps had ordered that two thirds of the allocation should be expended at night on harassing fire on roads. *As most of our batteries had little flash cover, such shooting betrayed our gun positions. Recourse was, therefore, had to single guns firing from night positions, pushed forward at dusk and withdrawn at dawn. Some of these forward guns had an unpleasant reception. One was destroyed by accurate enemy fire. The Germans, for their part, paid greater attention to our batteries than to our trenches. Their favourite method was deliberately shooting up a single battery, beginning with aeroplane observation and continued with high shrapnel bursts for about five or six hours at a round a minute. These bombardments caused some damage and some loss to the guns.*[108]

Although (according to intelligence sources) the German 54th Division and some units of the Landwehr division were supported by only 34 guns, from 15 September onwards Claud's batteries came

[107] General Sir Frederick Pile commanded Anti-Aircraft Command in the Second World War. He describes a wartime steeplechase in his autobiography. Judging by his account of the unruly behaviour of the riders, it may well have been the same steeplechase.

[108] SOS targets were targets on which an urgent response was required such as the approaches to a vulnerable trench. They were agreed with the infantry and registered in advance. If there was only one, the guns were laid on the target when not engaged elsewhere. If the infantry needed the immediate response for an SOS target, all they had to do was fire a verey light of an agreed colour and a sentry on the gun position could fire the first round before waking the detachments. One of the gunners is buried in the small cemetery just outside the village.

under sustained artillery fire day after day. On the 22 September B Battery was shelled intermittently all day with 5.9s. At Gale's battery (Major H D Gale MC RFA) a delayed action 5.9 shell penetrated the mine dugout to a depth of 20 feet before exploding, killing three soldiers and wounding seven, including Gale. *He and McMillan did fine work rescuing men from the mine during heavy shelling.* [109]

Next day Metz was shelled. The stable for Claud's horse Sandy was in danger. He got the horses out just in time before the next shell demolished the adjoining building. He decided the headquarters staff must excavate a dugout.

Three days later it was the howitzer battery's turn to be straffed all day from 10.30 am until 8 pm with about 350 rounds of 5.9s. Claud attempted to visit them during a lull but, before he arrived at the gun position, the shelling began again. He watched from behind a tree about 150 yards away. The German gunners were very accurate, using new instantaneous fuses. When the shelling eased he went to see the damage, *one gun slightly damaged, three gun pits destroyed as well as the cookhouse. In fact the whole place was an awful mess.*

On 27 September Claud spent the day watching the howitzers being calibrated at Fricourt, just east of Albert, one of the two Third Army calibration ranges. He returned to Metz to find the village and C Battery had been under heavy shellfire all day. None of the gunners had been hit but two guns and much ammunition had been destroyed and six infantrymen killed when a shell hit their billet. The battery was deployed to a new location, and Claud spent an evening helping with the excavation of the headquarters dugout. A lone gun deployed forward by A Battery came under prolonged bombardment by 5.9s, one of which had hit the shield, reducing the gun to a heap of scrap metal.

By now the diary entries had been reduced to comments on the weather *filthy* but an exciting incident on 13 November he described in full.

To new positions in morning and to C Battery. Whilst there saw a 'plane very low in the mist. He looked like a Hun and when archies

---

[109] Falls, ibid p. 133

turned on him, my suspicions confirmed. When archies opened he turned away and was headed off by machine guns and turned towards where I was standing. Came dead straight at me descending all the time and eventually landed 20 to 30 yards away. I ran up with Sergeant Rayner and we took the Hun prisoner. He was a bit shaken by the landing and 'hands up' at once before he could burn the machine. Though his propeller was broken and the undercarriage part of the machine smashed through catching the bank alongside the road, the engine etc were entirely undamaged. We took him off to C's mess and gave him drinks, smokes and tea. He was awfully fed up at first but soon revived. Had ascended at Laon, got lost in the mist after a fight and eventually had to come down owing to having no petrol left. Another 300 yards and he would have been safe behind the Bosch lines. He was an officer, a Pole, and spoke a little French but no English. 'Plane a lovely new single seater Albatros Scout of latest pattern; only left factory in October. Two fixed machine guns firing through propeller. Eventually APM IV Corps took him over whilst 15 Squadron RFC removed the 'plane. Being only a month old, it must have been of great intelligence interest to the Royal Flying Corps.

Once Haig had approved the plan in mid October, the preparations for the coming battle went ahead. The attack was to be carried out by three corps of Third Army, IV Corps on the left, III Corps on the right and V Corps in reserve. IV Corps would be composed of three divisions, 36th on the left, 62nd at the centre and 51st on the right. On the night 17/18 November, 51st Division and 62nd Division took over the front line that had been held by the brigades of 36th Division since late August. Only 109th Infantry Brigade from 36th Division was to have a role in the initial assault, attacking northwards from Spoil Heap, rolling up the Hindenburg Line on the west bank of the canal.

Assembling the force without revealing the preparations to the enemy was an enormous undertaking. It had to be carried out almost entirely by night; movement by day was forbidden. Fortunately the weather, a thick ground mist lingering all day, provided additional cover. For the first fortnight in November 200 to 600 men from 36th Division were employed unloading ammunition trains at Ytres railhead. Ammunition in large quantities, 700 rounds per field gun, had to be dumped at present and probable future gun positions. The concentration of the artillery, over 1,000 pieces, began on the

7 November and was completed on the night of 17/18 November, field, heavy and siege brigades arriving from the north, interspersed with infantry and cavalry units and ammunition columns. 350 battle tanks moved into Havrincourt Wood, which was already crammed with small hutments. Heavy lorries and small steamrollers carried out repairs to the roads, especially the rides through the wood, and piles of hardcore were dumped for future use. Portable bridges were made to enable the guns to cross both the British and the particularly wide trenches of the Hindenburg Line. And everything that had been achieved under darkness had to be camouflaged by dawn.

In the early hours of 20 November, like a great beast awakening, the battalions and tanks along the whole of the two corps fronts moved forward into their attack positions, the noise of their movement covered by long bursts of machine gun fire. How the Germans had remained oblivious to all these preparations for a month seems almost miraculous, yet the attack at 6.20 am, preceded by the opening of the fire plan, came as a complete surprise.

The attack was an enormous success. Despite some doubts about the accuracy of targets that had not been registered in advance, the artillery support was described by the infantry as magnificent. By the end of the first day divisions had advanced five miles. The 'impenetrable' Hindenburg defence works had been overrun, the greater part of the area between the Canal du Nord and the Canal de l'Escaut had been cleared and a bridgehead established over the latter by a bridge that had not been blown. The only check had been at Flesquières where 51st Division failed to provide the close infantry support for the tanks, with the result that eleven were knocked out by the German gunners who, exceptionally in this division, had been trained in engaging these new weapons over open sights at point-blank range. As a result this attack at the centre was called off for the day. In London the bells rang to celebrate a great victory, the good news that the nation needed to counter the doom coming from Passchendaele.

153rd Brigade, having participated in the fire plan in support of 62nd Division, left Havrincourt Wood at midnight to rejoin its parent division by way of Metz (passing the cottage of the halcyon days), Ruyalcourt, Hermies and Demicourt. The narrow roads were congested. It was not until 7.30 am on 21 November that the batteries moved into their new positions 2,000 yards north east of Demicourt, with the headquarters in the old front line 1,000 yards due east of the village. The attack by 109th Brigade on the previous day had gone well, rolling up the German defences west of the canal and had consolidated on the Bapaume-Cambrai road, with outposts 300-400 yards to the north. Casualties had been exceptionally light.

On the following day progress in the salient now formed as a result of the previous days' advances, was less successful. Flesquières fell and the advance continued to Bourlon Wood, but there the attack stalled. Bourlon, the ridge which overlooked the greater part of the battlefield, the village and the wood were vital to success. If they could be taken then the way would be open for the cavalry to exploit towards the Sensée. Fatally, the divisions that had fought so splendidly on the first day stopped on reaching their objectives instead of exploiting their success. The tank crews were worn out. In the first version tanks the ventilation was so bad that it was reckoned a crew took 30 hours to recuperate after a day in their machines. The new model was not much better. By chance, unknown to the corps staff, a German division, released from the Russian front, had arrived at Cambrai station the night before the British attack, in time to reinforce the 54th and Landwehr divisions. Had the British only realised it, there was still a wide gap where the bridgehead had been established over the Canal de l'Escaut south of Cambrai and for hours the way to that town was wide open. Now it was too late. German reinforcements had arrived with commendable speed. Within days the weight of their artillery fire had greatly increased. To add to the discomfort of the troops, the high winds and downpours of rain were threatening to turn to snow.

In the early hours of 22 November, 109th Brigade was relieved and the other two brigades of 36th Division brought into the line. East of the canal 107th Brigade was to clear the first and second lines of the Hindenburg support trenches, whilst 108th Brigade took Moeuvres on the west bank of the canal. The attack took place mid morning after a 40 minute barrage. For the first time in the battle the Division was to be supported by tanks, but they were not much help. Of the eleven that started out, one was ditched at the outset, one turned the wrong way and was not seen again, six were knocked out by artillery fire and only three remained at the end of the day. 108th Brigade succeeded in breaking into the village, but communications between the brigade and the artillery had broken down, probably as a result of the tanks cutting the telephone cables. Not knowing how far the infantry had advanced, the batteries were unable to provide fire support. At the end of the afternoon the Germans mounted a strong counter attack and the brigade was forced to withdraw to its start line.

For a week the battle for Bourlon raged, attack met by counter attack, village and wood changing hands until the hopes of a breakout were abandoned. On 23 November IV Corps mounted a co-ordinated attack northwards that met with some success. Bourlon Wood was captured but lost again the following day. 36th Division again attacked astride the canal, reaching Moeuvres once more, but at dusk the brigade was forced to withdraw to the southern outskirts of the village.

107th Brigade was to renew the assault on the following day, but the day began with a violent German assault on Bourlon Wood and the 36th Divisional artillery had to be diverted to the Bourlon SOS targets.[110] The batteries came under heavy hostile fire directed from observation aircraft. There was hardly any cover from view, with the result that two guns were destroyed and nine men killed or wounded. Left without artillery support, the planned attack by 107th Brigade was called off.[111]

That night, 26 November, the 36th (Ulster) Division was relieved by 2nd Division, leaving its two artillery brigades still in action south of Moeuvres. "That night will remain an unpleasant memory to the survivors of the troops who were then relieved," Falls wrote five years later. "The snow had come now and swept almost horizontally before a wind that at times rose to tempestuous force. The relief took a very long time. When it was over the men staggered through the blizzard to very indifferent havens that were to be their lodgings for the night.... A good many men spent what was left of the night in the open in the snow." The following day the division moved further west to the more congenial area south east of Bapaume where they waited, so they understood, for orders to move to a relatively quiet sector east of Arras.

---

[110] See Footnote 108
[111] Falls, ibid p.166

Photograph © Imperial War Museum (Q9347)

This may be one of the guns of 153rd Brigade crossing the Canal du Nord which was still under construction – the southern section had not yet been flooded.

Meanwhile Claud moved his headquarters to a position by Lock 7. The guns spent the night on harassing fire with 50 rounds per gun. In the early hours B and C Batteries took up new positions, just east of the canal.[112]

On 30 November, shortly after daylight, the great German counter offensive began, directed simultaneously on the north and south of the British salient. In the north the assault came mainly from the direction of Bourlon. It met with near total failure. Not since the early days of the war had the British artillery and machine guns seen such targets. The 153rd Brigade war diary records that "many large parties of Germans were caught in the open by artillery fire. 153rd Brigade fired SOS barrage throughout the day, expending about 10,000 rounds. Attack was completely repulsed by machine gun and artillery fire. It is estimated that two German divisions were annihilated. Many aeroplane encounters took place during the day

[112] See photograph

resulting in the downfall of several machines on both sides. Brigade suffered no casualties." In a phrase reminiscent of the BBC in years to come, the final diary entry for that historic day reads "normal conditions resumed about 6.30 pm."

Claud watched the attack from a rise beside his battery deployed at Lock 7. At the end of the day he found time to write to his mother a vivid description of the battle: *The Huns came on in dense masses, wave after wave of them in full view in the open and accompanied by guns. Our artillery had fine targets and fairly straffed them.* [Some guns of 173rd Brigade were moved up onto a ridge to engage the German guns over open sights]. *A very large number of his men were bowled over. It is impossible to estimate the size of the attack but I myself have seen many thousands. I've never seen anything like it before during the war. The whole thing was most thrilling and when I saw our infantry up and counter attack, I could scarcely contain myself and longed to pick up a gun and bayonet and go after them. The shelling was fairly heavy all day and I had a few most unpleasantly close but while one was excited at watching our guns getting onto the Hun little trifles like hostile shelling are hardly noticed. We had only a few fellows knocked over and taken all round we were extremely lucky.*

Aircraft were very active all day and this afternoon I saw a colossal air battle in which 50 or 60 planes took part. Several were downed on both sides, but on the whole, though we were considerably superior in numbers, it seems that Fritz got rather the better of things. I also saw one of our observation balloons brought down today and another yesterday. They well deserved this success as in both cases they made straight for the balloons and downed them. The sausage men got clear by parachute.

We've had a pretty stiff time the last ten days. We have been cold, wet and dirty, spent many nights without sleep and been generally uncomfortable. But when you are beating the Hun it doesn't matter. The men have kept extraordinarily cheerful in spite of many discomforts and I was ever so pleased with them.

The lovely warm socks his mother had sent could not have arrived at a more opportune time. At the time the parcel arrived *we were living in a trench with a bit of corrugated iron on top. It was alternately snowing and pouring with rain. What with the mud, the drips, the cold and the filth we were not feeling our best. Now we are in a Bosch dugout in the Hindenburg Line and, though it is very dirty and the accommodation somewhat limited, it is anyhow warm and dry and what is still more important uncommonly safe!*

Whilst the German attack in the north of the salient had made little progress, those in the south and south east were far more threatening. III Corps, the right hand British corps, was not deployed for a defensive battle and was short of artillery. Many of the batteries were taken by surprise and overrun. 60 field and howitzer guns were lost. The Germans broke through and at their furthest point reached Gouzeaucourt, 2,000 yards beyond the original British front line. It was largely the gunners who saved the day, fighting with great gallantry. A subaltern and a sergeant were awarded Victoria Crosses.

Since being relieved on 29 November, the day before the German counter offensive, the infantry brigades of 36th Division had suffered a very difficult period. Initially they had been told that they were being sent to a quiet area near Arras. Advance parties had already gone north to select billets. Then, in the afternoon, came news of the German attack in the south, and the orders were changed. The division was placed at the disposal of the beleaguered III Corps and ordered to take over part of the front line between Beaucamp and Villers Pluich. For the battalions, their men worn out by ten days of fighting, it must have come as a bitter disappointment. The situation in the south was critical, the rear areas were under heavy bombardment by artillery and from the air. Little Metz, including the cottage, was bombed day and night, and Havrincourt Wood was rendered uninhabitable by its constant shelling.

"Never since it landed in France had the troops of 36th Division been rendered to such a physical ebb so low. The men became indescribably dirty; lungs, throat and heart were affected... the troops had, in fact, been exposed to three weeks of winter in the open, with almost continuous fighting, while it is doubtful whether they had fully recovered from the effects of the Ypres episode three months earlier." [113]

---

[113]   Falls, ibid p.177

The 36th (Ulster) Division was the only formation to have been committed to both halves of the Cambrai salient. They could no longer go on. On the night of 14/15 December they were relieved by the Royal Navy Division and sent to a rest area at Lucheux, north east of Doullens.

On 3 December the Germans called off their attack. Like the British in the north, they had created a salient in which they were in danger of being cut off. Next day Haig ordered a withdrawal to the Hindenburg support line across the whole front. The Battle of Cambrai was over. Honours were about even on both sides. Each had gained and lost a similar area of territory. Third Army had had 6,000 taken prisoner, the Germans 10,000. The total of killed, wounded and missing was more or less the same for both sides at about 45,000. The Germans had lost 138 guns, the British 158. From the British point of view, more important than the results, were the lessons learned, the use of tanks *en masse*, co-operation between infantry, tanks and artillery, and huge strides in the preparation and employment of the artillery without a preliminary barrage.

After the withdrawal of 36th Division, 153rd Brigade remained in action for a further ten days. The batteries were deployed in the Grande Ravine between Havrincourt and Ribecourt, coming under shell and gas attack, and frequently overflown by hostile aircraft flying absurdly low. *His planes seem to go anywhere and do what they like and are completely on top at the moment.*

Twice the brigade OP was shelled and a major and a subaltern killed. C Battery lost 40 horses. The howitzer battery came under shellfire and suffered ten casualties. On 5 December the batteries engaged many targets, inflicting heavy casualties on the enemy as they closed up to the old British front line. That night, in accordance with Haig's instructions for a general withdrawal, the brigade moved back to new positions south of Hermes. The following day the batteries began digging new positions. Each battery deployed a gun forwarded to an *almost open* position, whence it would be able to engage tanks if the Germans tried to use captured British machines. The brigade war diary reports that "a large number of enemy aeroplanes crossed over our lines, flying at very low altitudes. Formation consisted of a fighter escort of Scouts and one or two large bomb dropping machines. Met with no opposition either from AA guns or RFC. Formation proceeded to wagon lines and dropped large quantity of different sized bombs, again without interference by RFC. Formation eventually broke up and went home having suffered no casualties." Claud described one of the machines as *very large and double engines and on top of it someone seemed to be walking about.* [114]

On 14 December the brigade moved yet again, with gun positions in K30 outside Ribecourt, with the headquarters in a dugout in the Hindenburg support line. Claud told his mother that he was fed up with all those moves to *suit the idiosyncrasies of some persons sitting in comfort at Corps HQ.* He had only written the first page of his letter before they were moved again to another Hindenburg dugout, *very dirty and smelly but at least safe.*

Christmas Day passed quietly. On Boxing Day the brigade was relieved by the artillery of the Royal Navy Division and moved to a staging area in the sugar factory in Le Transloy. The brigade's troubles were not yet over.

All Northern France was snowbound. Trains suffered long delays, transport had to struggle up roads through drifts six feet and more in depth. Some roads simply could not be located. "Units were obliged to march miles off their course, bringing the vehicles through drifts in relays with double traces, trace horses being sent back for a second batch when the first was on firmer ground." [115]

For four days the batteries of 153rd Brigade were stuck in the Transloy sugar factory, waiting for a thaw before renewing their journey southwards into 1918 and the next great battle.

---

[114] Farndale records that in the southern flank attack up to 100 German aircraft were involved at one time, machine gunning and bombing the trenches, more aircraft than had ever been seen before in this role. Farndale, ibid p.250.

[115] Falls, ibid p.177

Chapter 11 LUDENDORFF'S SPRING OFFENSIVE March 1918

Nobody doubted that the Germans would mount a major offensive in the spring of 1918. Ludendorff, the German supreme commander, must have had one overruling aim, the defeat of the British and thereby the end of the war. Now it appeared he had his opportunity. The first units of the American Expeditionary Force had begun to arrive in France, but had to undergo further training before they would be fit for operations. Meanwhile, following the collapse of Russia, troop trains had been delivering divisions from the Eastern Front. By March, Ludendorff had 187 divisions at his disposal, compared with 178 from the British, French and Belgians.

Ludendorff chose for the first phase of his offensive, Operation 'Michael', the sector between Arras, St Quentin and the Oise. It was the Allies' weakest point, the junction between the British and the French. The ground offered few difficulties, apart from the latter stages where the armies would be crossing country laid waste in the Somme battles. It was to be carried out by three armies, a total of 63 divisions. Having achieved a breakthrough, two of the armies were to wheel northwards and force the British back to the Channel coast, whilst the Third Army would cover the left flank. 43 divisions would be launched against the British Fifth Army and 19 divisions against the six divisions of the Third Army. At his disposal for the offensive he would have a massive total of 6,473 guns of all calibres, plus 3,532 trench mortars, compared with 1,312 in support of the Fifth Army. [116]

---

[116] Farndale, ibid pp.261–262.

In January Haig warned the Government that the next four months would be the most critical of the war. The French were running out of manpower. The infantry establishment of their remaining divisions was half the number it had been in 1914. To relieve pressure on their allies and to achieve a more equitable division of the whole length of the western front, the British had agreed to extend their right flank from the River Somme to the River Oise, thereby taking over from the French an increased frontage of some 25 miles. Yet the British, too, were running out of manpower. Lloyd George had refused to release 600,000 trained soldiers available in the United Kingdom to be sent to France, concerned that they would be expended in a fruitless continuation of Passchendaele.

Since Cambrai the BEF had undergone a major reorganisation, with divisions being reduced to nine infantry battalions and brigades to three battalions. A substantial number [117] were disbanded or reduced to cadres, others inter-posted among divisions, to be separated from comrades they had served beside in past battles. The effect was damaging to morale, particularly in those divisions with territorial backgrounds. "The characteristics of the Ulster Division were entirely changed. Its infantry, formed originally from the Ulster Volunteer Force (UVF), had now Ulster Scot and Celt intermingled, and received English recruits as well." [118]

All the indications pointed to a German spring offensive. The only doubt was where would it fall. Haig's primary concern was to block the way to the Channel ports. He was well aware that, whilst all the armies were fully extended, Fifth Army holding the southern flank was particularly weak. However, he calculated that a breakthrough there would have no immediate strategic advantage in so far as Ludendorff's aim was to defeat the British and knock them out of the war. Accordingly, of the 18 divisions available for Haig to hold in reserve, half were held in the north and just three were available to the Fifth Army. The Fifth Army was made up of three corps: XVIII Corps, composed of 30th,

---

[117] There are different versions of the number of battalions lost; Falls says 175; Terraine "145 in France".

[118] Falls, ibid p.185. The modern Loyalist paramilitary terrorist organisation had no connection with the old UVF, other than copying its honourable name.

36th and 61st Divisions, which was holding the centre; XIX Corps was in the north; and III Corps held the southern boundary between the British and the French.

The Ulstermen had spent Christmas resting and refitting after the rigours of Cambrai. As soon as Christmas was over, they set out southwards by road and rail to take over the extended front from the French. The roads were still dangerous, blocked by deep drifts. William Carr, a gunner officer, who, though not a member of the 36th Division artillery, was deploying in the same general area, described the difficulties of moving horses and guns over roads in the grip of ice: "I've never seen anything like going down that hill out of Bergicourt. It was impossible to keep a foothold on the road. Horses just could not move without falling into a tangled heap. Imagine a team of six horses sprawling in the road mixed up with harness and a gun running into them. We fixed drag ropes on to wagons and limbers. At either side of the road two men hung on to each rope, struggling to keep a foothold in the snow. Eventually we managed to hold back the vehicles and coaxed the horses down the hill. The drivers suffered most. Up on horseback they caught the full force of the icy blast. Without any orders gunners offered to take their places, so that life could be restored to frozen limbs." [119]

36th Division spent four days resting at Corbie, where they were rejoined by the divisional artillery before moving slowly onwards to Nesle. So far the town was relatively undamaged and many of the townspeople were still in residence. Divisional headquarters was set up in the town by 12 January and by 15 January the infantry and artillery brigades had taken over from their French counterparts. Time was fast running out and there was much to be done. The French had made little effort to prepare defence works. Their trenches were little more than scrapes in the ground. The British had taken a leaf out of the German military manual, adopting the system of defence in depth that had served them so well at Passchendaele: a forward zone consisting of outposts, a line of resistance and a counter attack company; a battle zone 2,300 yards deep; and a rear zone, which, in the present instance, consisted of little more than a line on the map.

---

[119] *A Time to Leave the Ploughshares*, William Carr, p.84.

On the 36th Division front there were six redoubts, three in the forward zone and three in the battle zone, each held by a battalion in strong defence works surrounded by wire. As a result of the division being over extended, none of them was able to support each other. The system depended on reliable communications via telephone lines dug into the ground, but these were soon to be broken by shellfire. As yet there were few wirelesses.

The gunner batteries were ordered to select alternative positions and single gun positions sited to engage tanks, another leaf from the German manual.[120] Guns positioned within 3,000 yards of the front were to be wired in and prepared for all round defence and to serve as rallying points for withdrawing infantry. To this end, each battery was issued with a Lewis gun.[121]

The divisional artillery had been reinforced. 179th Army Field Brigade supported 109th Infantry Brigade on the left. 173rd Brigade made up the right group covering the other two infantry brigades. Claud's 153rd Brigade provided cover over the battle zone.

At some time between Christmas and 6 February, Claud had gone home on leave. There is no record of how long he had been away, though he told his mother earlier that he hoped to be given a month. Whether he took part in the winter march to Corbie and then to the new brigade positions deployed south west of St Quentin, there is now sadly no way of knowing. In a new volume of his diary he recorded his journey back to war. *Arrived Boulogne 4.30. To 'movies'* [a surprising Americanism]. *Dinner 7.30 at The Metropole. Left Boulogne at 10.15. Arrived Ham 9.30* [the following morning] *after quite a comfortable journey. Rode to Brigade HQ arriving ¼ to 12. Good accommodation recently taken over from the French. Round some of the batteries. All very quiet on this Front but*

---

[120] The Germans did use captured British tanks salvaged from earlier battles. At the battle of Villers Bretonneux, east of Amiens, on 5 April the first tank battle in history took place when 3 British Heavy Mark IVs supported by the new medium Whippets engaged 4 German A7Vs. They weighed 33 tons and were heavy and clumsy, designed to carry a crew of eighteen. Only 15 of the machines had been brought into service by the end of the war.

[121] Farndale, ibid p.259

everybody has wind up over expected Hun attack. Batteries working like fiends on positions.[122]

February passed with no sign of an impending attack apart from increased air activity. Almost every day Claud was going round the batteries, checking up on progress on the defence works at the gun positions, selecting alternative OPs and gun positions to cover all approaches and single guns to be occupied in the event of attacks by tanks. Usually he rode round the battle zone on a bicycle, on one occasion a 16-mile pedal to Ham and back to attend the corps commander's talk on lessons from Cambrai. On ordinary roads it would not have been far, but on roads churned up by heavy traffic, it was hard going.

Apart from carrying out calibration, the guns were for the most part silent, not least because persistent mist made observation of fire almost impossible. Fire was directed at enemy working parties if they were more than 20 strong. On 11 February the brigade war diary recorded "small groups of enemy seen conducting themselves in a singular manner, really doing nothing but attempting to appear most industrious. Others were purely pushing wheel barrows round a field in a circle for two hours without a load. A large working party was engaged by our 18 pounders with effect." What they were doing one can only surmise. Drawing the fire of the guns so that the locations of individual gun positions could be revealed? Or creating an impression that these activities were purely defensive and that there were no plans for an attack on this front?

On 20 February the brigade was relieved and moved back to Offoy on the Somme, two miles north west of Ham, to undergo training consisting of gun drill, signalling and riding drills. The village was not much damaged and many of the villagers were still living in their homes. The accommodation was good, *a Mess with a piano, a comfortable bed-sitting room, and a very nice old lady as hostess.* Claud took the opportunity to visit the airfield at nearby Matigny occupied by 23 Squadron, Royal Flying Corps, equipped with SE5s and French manufactured Spads.[123] On 28 February orders were

---

[122] According to the brigade war diary, the gun positions were at Sheet 66, F22d, 200 yards east of Contescourt.

[123] A week later the Royal Flying Corps was retitled the Royal Air Force.

received to man the battle zone positions with brigade HQ at Grand Seraucourt and battery gun positions as follows: A Battery G8d 9.5; B Battery G15a 9.9 and L5a 7.7; C Battery L4a 4.4 and G9b 0.5; and D Battery 9b 5.5 and L12e 9.11.[124]

For the first fortnight in March there was still no firm intelligence about the Germans' intentions. The air forces on both sides were active, the Germans carrying out bombing raids on the rear areas. Claud counted 20 Albatrosses in one formation. After a week of rain, snow and bitter east winds, the weather suddenly changed. Nights of frost were followed by warm, even hot summer-like days, day after day, bringing on the spring flowers, the trees budding and the men becoming sunburnt. By 17 March there were indications, particularly the noise of enemy movement along the roads by night, that dispelled any lingering doubts about where the attack was to take place. Like the boxer waiting to go into the ring knowing that he will be outclassed, the men of the Third and Fifth Armies waited for the blow to fall. On 18 March two deserters stated that the attack was to take place in three days on 21 March. Prisoners taken in a raid that night confirmed the date. In the early hours the British guns bombarded the likely forming up areas.

The German army had developed tactics that were to be the forerunner of the *blitzkreig* that swept the Wehrmacht through Belgium and into France in the early summer of 1940. Masses of artillery were concentrated in secrecy close to the front line, prepared to bombard the enemy defences without any preliminary registration. Lightly equipped storm-troopers, armed only with rifles, machine guns and light mortars and without their own artillery support, were trained to press ahead with all speed, infiltrating the enemy defences and leaving his strong points to be dealt with in detail by the following infantry.

At 4.35 am on 21 March, the German offensive began with a bombardment of unprecedented weight, three million shells in three hours, including thousands of shells of phosgene gas. For the first two hours the main weight of fire was directed against the British gun positions. Despite the fact that there had been no previous

---

[124] All references refer to the 1:40,000 Sheet 66. Each battery, less A Battery, had deployed a section forward into anti-tank positions.

registration, the fire was deadly accurate and, due to the weather conditions, heat and mist, the gas did not disperse but lingered in the valleys and hollows. "Think of the loudest clap of thunder you have ever heard," Carr wrote, "then imagine what it would be like if it continued without stopping. I have never before nor since heard anything like it. We groped for candles and turned out of bed. With coats over our pyjamas we rushed outside. We turned towards the line, a fiery glow to right and left. Visibility was ten yards at the most. It was impossible to talk or even shout. The noise made us almost stupid." [125]

After two hours the hostile fire switched to the forward infantry positions, using mainly trench mortars. Howitzers and long-range guns concentrated on the rear areas and the crossings over the Crozat canal. Very quickly communications between headquarters and the forward areas and gun positions were lost. To add to the confusion the mist, though usual at that time of year, was particularly dense that morning and did not begin to lift until the afternoon. The British guns, out of touch with their OPs, unable to see visual signals, hampered by wearing gas masks, responded so far as they could to the infantry's DF tasks. In many cases they engaged the advancing hordes over open sights at point blank range. Indeed many did not even know the attack had begun until they saw the grey clad storm-troopers coming out of the mist, closing in on their gun positions.

The layout of the defences of 36th Division with 108th Brigade on the right flank, adjacent to the left flank of 14th Division of III Corps, rendered the Ulster Division particularly vulnerable to being outflanked. When about 8.30 am the storm-troopers advanced, their attack came not on the 36th Division's front line, but on the right flank of the battalions manning the forward defences. Despite gallant and costly resistance, they were soon overwhelmed. By midday the division's 173rd Artillery Brigade, forming the right group, came under machine gun and rifle fire at close range. The detachments were forced to abandon their guns, having first removed the breech blocks and dial sights.

The storm-troopers exploited the gaps between the redoubts, advancing as far as Contescourt, a distance of 4,500 yards behind

---

[125] Carr, ibid p.98

the British front line at the start of the day. They made even greater progress on the 14th Division front, forcing 108th Brigade to retire to new positions on the railway line west of Essigny. By late afternoon the three redoubts on the 36th Division forward zone, cut off and surrounded after an epic defence, had been forced to surrender. As a result the three brigades had each lost a battalion, a third of their strength, on the first day of the battle.

At the outset of the day Claud had his headquarters in a dugout in Grand Seraucourt, sharing it with the staff of 107th Brigade in accordance with the pre-battle orders that the infantry and artillery headquarters should be as close as possible to each other. Since the bombardment began, most of the buried wires had been cut and, throughout the day, the two headquarters had little idea of what was happening in their battalions and batteries, apart from the information that runners could bring in and a tenuous system of telephone wires within the battle zone. In the evening, following the loss of 173rd Brigade, the divisional artillery was reorganised. Claud took over command of the right group, consisting of his own A and B Batteries, the howitzer battery of 173rd and a battery of 91st Artillery Brigade from 20th Division, one of the three reserve divisions in Fifth Army that had been ordered forward to cover the boundary between III Corps and XVII Corps.

By now the Germans had made considerable progress on the 14th Division front, leaving the right flank of the 36th (Ulster) Division dangerously exposed. They were closing in on Grand Seraucourt. Orders were given that the headquarters of 107th Brigade and 153rd Artillery Brigade were to withdraw to a new location alongside B Battery. The order came none too soon. As they moved out, machine gun fire was coming down the village street. By the time they reached the new location, fresh orders had come in. The army commander had ordered III Corps to withdraw behind the canal. 36th Division had to conform. Claud was to collect his batteries, cross to the west bank of the Crozat canal and come into action between Bray St Christophe and Tugny. With great difficulty the guns were assembled and, after a long night march, came into action by 5 am, with the headquarters alongside 108th Brigade in Bray. *A very straining and tiring 24 hours,* Claud concluded his diary entry for the day. *The Hun has begun well and had the luck of the devil with the weather*. On that first day alone the British had suffered 38,000 casualties, of whom 21,000 were taken prisoner.

"So ended the 21st March 1918, one of the blackest days in the history of the British army," Farndale writes. "But all was not lost. Thanks to the gallantry of gunners and infantrymen the tenuous line had held. Ludendorff was bitterly disappointed. His casualties were far higher than he had envisaged. His losses in officers and junior leaders were so high that we now know that the German army was never able to recover." [126]

Claud's diary for 22 March tells of order, counter-order and growing confusion. No sooner had he set up his headquarters in Bray than he was ordered to take up new positions west of that village and in the vicinity of Aubigny. His task was to support 108th Brigade, which had been joined by the survivors of 'Ricardo', the last of the redoubts to be overrun. The brigade was holding a line between Happencourt and Fluquieres. The morning passed relatively quietly. At 2 pm Claud was ordered to move back with commander 108th Brigade to Pithon. On arriving there he was told that his group was to come under command of 20th Division Artillery. This presented great difficulty as he had lost contact with the batteries, three of which had misunderstood their orders and moved back to Offoy, west of Ham. He sent out his adjutant, intelligence officer, runners and signallers to look for them but without success. About 7 pm he was ordered to deploy with the remaining batteries at Eppeville, just outside Ham but south of the river. Passing through Ham he found the missing batteries. New orders were received. He was to take the group, now six batteries, along the Ham/Nesle road and come into action at Bacquencourt to cover the crossings across the Somme. They arrived about 3 am and all batteries were in action by dawn, affiliated to 61st Infantry Brigade of 20th Division. It had been a very long day. The mist had returned in the morning, clearing to a glorious day, but the move through the night had been terribly cold.

Next morning, 23 March, news came through that the Germans were across the Somme at Ham and were advancing on Esmery-Hallon. Claud was ordered to move his group by way of Breuil, Moyencourt and Ercheu to Libermont and to await orders there.

---

[126] Farndale, ibid p.265

Whilst the batteries prepared to move, he collected his battery commanders and rode ahead to the headquarters of the divisional artillery in Freniches to find out more precisely what his group was to do and to select gun positions. The roads were packed with guns, lorries and transport, intermingled with French civilians with their belongings on carts and barrows, all moving back from the Somme. The scene was that of a great retreat, but fairly orderly, although there was a jam at Libermont bridge. The group was instructed to occupy positions between Fréniches and Libermont.

For the moment there was a pause in the action, providing an opportunity to exchange horses with 173rd Brigade which, having lost most of their guns on the first morning, were now non-operational. Some time in the afternoon (by now not surprisingly Claud has forgotten the times when writing up his diary) the group was ordered to come into action in the area of Flavy-Le-Meldeux, east of Libremont, to cover the road running south from Ham through Golancourt to Guiscard. Again Claud went ahead with the BCs. On the way they were machine gunned by three enemy aircraft flying low up and down the road. They took refuge in a small mud hut but, when one of the aeroplanes began dropping bombs, they had to scatter to more substantial cover, in Claud's case *a very nice place under a hand cart*. Two soldiers from B Battery had been wounded, one of them seriously.

The group deployed into its new positions just before dusk. Units from a French division came up to support them, but they were without artillery and had no more small arms ammunition other than what each soldier could carry.

It had been another long, tiring day. After two nights without sleep, men and horses were worn out. At last they had a chance to rest. Claud put his head down around 10 pm, but not for long. All that day 107th Brigade and 61st Brigade of 20th Division had been conducting a fighting withdrawal against the Germans, who had fought their way over the southern arm of the Crozat canal. By evening they were in Cugny, five miles to the east of the group's positions. Around 3.30 am on 24 March *an excited infantry officer* ran in to the brigade headquarters with a warning that the Germans had taken Golancourt and were coming down the Guiscard road and would be on top of the brigade in a few minutes. Sounds of machine gun and rifle fire confirmed the warning. The guns were brought out of action and moved half a mile down the road to Fréniches and formed up, awaiting events. The fog had closed in again with visibility reduced to a hundred yards. About 7 am the information was confirmed, the Germans were in Golancourt.

153rd Brigade, now referred to as the 'Potter Group', returned to its positions at Flavy and, together with the Eley group, the other group in the 36th Division artillery, brought fire down on the roads running south from the Somme. Despite the fact that lack of communication made coordinated artillery fire very difficult, the Potter Group bombarded the enemy massing for attack in the neighbourhood of the Esmery-Hallon-Golancourt road, causing considerable casualties amongst the enemy troops out in the open.

By 11 am the Germans had been able to make progress on the left flank and the group was ordered to withdraw by batteries a section at a time, coming into action between Flavy and Fréniches. However, the group's right flank was under threat when 14th Division, the left hand formation of III Corps, gave way before the German advance. 14th Division had not distinguished itself on the first morning when its withdrawal allowed the Germans to attack the 36th (Ulster) Division in the flank and morale was low. By afternoon the enemy had reached Berlancourt and Claud's group had to move back to positions just in front of Fréniches for the night, with its headquarters in the village.

By now the French divisions were arriving in increasing numbers to take over the right flank of Fifth Army from the exhausted British battalions. The French general, Noyelle, had assumed command of all the formations south of the Somme. 36th Division, or what little was left of it, came under command of the French 62nd Division, which ordered it to withdraw westwards for 15 miles for reorganisation. As a result a wide gap developed between the British and the French in the area of Roye and was exploited by the Germans. More French reinforcements were due to arrive by train on the Amiens-Montdidier line. If the Germans could get there first and cut the line, the effect would be disastrous. Together 30th and 36th Divisions, exhausted as they were, managed to hold west of Roye for 36 hours until relieved by the French. They then continued their journey westwards over

the Avre to Sourdon. On 30 March they entrained at Saleux south of   **145**
Amiens. By 4 April they had travelled north, back to their familiar
stamping ground of the Ypres salient. The three infantry brigades
had been decimated. 108th Brigade was reduced to little over 300.
Total divisional casualties amounted to 7,252. Of these 185 officers
and 5,659 other ranks were reported as missing. Some four fifths of
the missing were prisoners, wounded and unwounded. Overall there
was very little left of the 36th (Ulster) Division.

Meanwhile the divisional artillery, organised in the two groups,
under their own divisional headquarters, had been put at the disposal
of the French. Over a month was to pass before they caught up with
their own division again, around Poperinghe, far to the north.

Claud was just settling down to a few hours sleep at Freniches when
he received orders that his group was to move during the night to
a position in front of Beaulieu in support of the French, who were
holding the line of the Somme-Libermont canal. Around midnight
he set out with his headquarters along roads crammed with horse and
motor transport moving back, the batteries following on. Around
3.30 am he set up his headquarters in a farm Fonds Gamet (U15).
Dead beat and very cold, he dossed down on bales of hay for a few
hours sleep in what was left of the night.

At 7 am on the following day, 25 March, Claud awoke to find that
the headquarters was surrounded by French batteries, and that
the British infantry brigades had gone. Heavy fighting was taking
place just to the north as the Germans attacked Libremont in great
strength. After being beaten back several times, losing large numbers
of men, they eventually forced a crossing at Moyencourt and, to
avoid being outflanked, the French retired behind the canal. By
1 pm the batteries were ordered to move back, taking up positions
in square U19c, immediately behind Beaulieu, coming into action in
a hollow with very little cover and difficult to get out of, with the
headquarters at Bouvresse Farm (T23a). Claud went back with the
battery commanders to select the positions. The village square in
Beaulieu was jammed with French guns and transport, a lucrative
target for the German artillery, but, for some reason, probably because
it was not deployed far enough forward to keep pace with the storm-
troopers, their guns were not much used to harass the retreating allies.

Having selected the new positions, Claud went back to his headquarters to find that they had already gone. With no means of communicating with them, he stayed a while to watch the French carry out a very professional withdrawal behind the canal. When he rode back to his batteries, he found his headquarters had set up in the ruins of Bouvresse Farm. There they were joined by Lieutenant Colonel Eley's group and later by three French batteries of 155mm guns coming into action round the farm.

Three hours later the two groups were ordered to withdraw two miles, with the headquarters in Avricourt, just south of the Roye-Noyon road. The German storm-troopers were following up fast. A Battery got away only just in time. No sooner had the batteries arrived than they were ordered to move further to the south. Claud was back on the road again with the battery representatives at midnight and selected positions in the Bois le Comte, two miles west of Candor (B15). It was wild rough country and they had difficulty following indifferent maps.[127] With no sign of his headquarters arriving, Claud returned to Avricourt to find out what was keeping them, but they had already gone. The German machine guns sounded pretty close. C Battery was just leaving. Claud joined them but after he had followed the gun teams across rough country tracks into what was apparently an impenetrable marsh, he struck off on his own and eventually came across the headquarters in a hovel 500 yards from Balny (B14d). Despite the difficulties of a move in darkness using inaccurate maps over marshy ground, all the batteries were in action by 5.30 am on 25 March.

Claud slept for an hour, to be woken by an urgent message from the divisional headquarters, that the French Division had withdrawn during the night but had forgotten to warn the British artillery groups. The divisional commander was most apologetic, imagining that by now the British gunners had probably been taken prisoner. The Germans had taken Cadnor and were in the woods just in front of the battery positions. The guns must clear out at once. Claud sent out officer patrols to confirm the enemy's actual locations and to check out the road towards Lassigny, Gury and Roye-sur-Matz.

[127] At least one of the map sheets covering the retreat, 66E, was only updated in March 1918. In many cases units did not have the appropriate maps, never having expected to need sheets so far to the west. An officer in a 60 pounder battery said he would have to use the Daily Mail war map if he was called on to provide indirect fire.

Within 20 minutes all the batteries were on the road and trotting down towards Lassigny, *a very fine performance considering they were in bad positions in open country, away from a decent road.* A huge column of guns, lorries and horse transport and fleeing civilians were moving down the road towards Roye-sur-Matz. It took two hours before the brigade could get through to the divisional artillery headquarters at Canny (G4). Eventually Claud found the CRA who ordered him to take his batteries southwards to Gury and wait there for further orders. Another huge column was coming down the road from Frèsnieres. Where the two columns met, there was considerable confusion and *things looked like assuming a disorderly retreat, especially as the Huns showed signs of following up pretty closely, especially from the north.* A few aircraft or long-range guns could have caused havoc but none appeared. The streams of troops and vehicles moved on, and the group formed up south of Gury, just inside the old French lines from the early days of the war. *Men and horses were just about done in and we got a very much needed three or four hours rest.* According to the war diary, "man and beast were watered and fed."

That afternoon the CRA, General Brock, who had just returned from leave, and the commander of the 77th French Division, to whom the British artillery had now been affiliated, held a conference with the artillery group commanders. The French had been hurriedly brought up from Compiegne and were to hold the wooded high ground immediately to the west of the Oise, dominating the approaches from the north. Claud's brigade was to cover the French right flank. By 11 pm two of the batteries were in position on the spur north of Chevincourt (T2); the other two, due to a misunderstanding of their orders, spent part of the night down in the valley at Elincourt and did not reach their correct positions until the early hours of the morning.

The night passed quietly, cold and brightly moonlit. The new positions in the old French front line from 1915/16 were still well wired, with an elaborate trench system and a huge view over the country to the north. Every move of the Germans could be observed. One of the OPs was up a 50-foot tree. However, the batteries had not been long settled in when a despatch rider brought orders from the CRA. Since Claud's group was out of communication with the divisional artillery headquarters and other units, it was to move across to the left flank of the division and come into action in the vicinity of St Claude Farm (M5c). *En route* they stopped in the valley at Chevincourt to water the horses and scavenge food for the men since no rations had arrived. They deployed into their new positions just in time to take part in a barrage which beat off a determined German attack. The remainder of the day and that night passed quietly, giving the batteries the rest they so desperately needed. *It has been a terrible 6 days and the men and horses are about done in. Poor old Sandy could hardly get along all day. I hope he isn't going to break up.*

Next day the Germans made several further attacks, notably up the valley west of the commanding feature of Plémont (H20), but on every occasion they were beaten back in disorder by extremely effective barrages.

Twelve miles to the northwest they had broken through, capturing the town of Mondidier, the furthest point of their offensive, 35 miles from their start line. Never again during the rest of the war were they to reach so far to the west, nor so close to Paris, close enough to bring up their 'Big Bertha' long-range gun to shell the capital. By now they were "as weary as the British and their morale was falling, surrenders increased, prisoners no longer showed their arrogance of the opening days of the great attack, depression had set in." [128] They had captured Albert, but in a complete breakdown in discipline, they had indulged in an orgy of drinking and looting, so intoxicated that when they attempted to push on next day they were mown down by British machine gunners. The loss of junior leaders in the early stages of the battle had begun to tell.

Amongst his gunners Claud noted a rise in morale after a good night's sleep and rumours that they were to be relieved in two days' time. Through its entire vicissitudes the brigade had remained intact with all its guns and equipment and had suffered very few casualties.

That evening the weather broke at last, heavy rain falling during the night. Had it come any sooner, the retreat across rough tracks and cross country would have been a greater nightmare.

---

[128] Farndale, ibid p.273

Good Friday, 29 March, was comparatively quiet. Claud walked up to the OP on Plémont hill (H20/21) and was amazed by the extent of the view. *With us holding this hill it should be very hard for the Hun to do anything, as every movement and the flash of every gun should be spotted.*

Next day the Germans renewed their attacks in considerable force along the fronts of the French 53rd and 77th Divisions, capturing Plessie-de-Roye (G24b) and advancing to within a few hundred yards of C Battery's gun position. One of the officers was cut off in his OP and had to fight his way out, firing 30 rounds from his revolver and claiming to have shot ten Germans. As a bonus he 'captured' a dozen French soldiers with their machine guns who insisted on surrendering to him in the belief that he was a German!

About midday, when the enemy was seen coming out of the wood in front of the gun position, Claud ordered C and D Batteries to withdraw back to St Claude farm. The gun positions and wagon line came under heavy shell fire. A Battery lost 25 horses, B Battery 18, and a number of gunners were wounded. At 5.30 pm the French counter attacked, splendidly supported by the 36th Divisional artillery, restoring the original line and taking 700 prisoners.

For the two artillery brigades it was the end of the great retreat now that the French had stabilised the situation. According to Falls the two brigades "had carried out a great task in a manner worthy of the highest traditions of the Royal Regiment." [129] At 9 pm they were withdrawn and marched through the night to Grand Fresnoy eight miles west of Compiegne. On arrival at 5.30 am they found that no arrangements had been made to provide billets and the batteries had to doss down wherever they could. William Carr, whose battery was following much the same route as the Ulster gunners, wrote of those final days. "Our destination was Chevincourt, far south of Gury and out of the battle zone. The road was as chaotic as ever. We moved slowly, our pace set by the vehicles ahead. At Lassigny we turned south. At last we were clear of the traffic but we and our horses were so worn that we couldn't move any faster. It was so cold it was agony to stop but we couldn't keep going without a frequent halt when the

---

[129] Falls, ibid p.229

gunners lay down by the side of the road and drivers slumped in their saddles. Every now and then the drivers and gunners changed places. I could only ride a short distance without falling asleep. We staggered forward in a daze, so exhausted that it was impossible to tell whether we were halted or on the move. When daylight dawned on Friday 29 March, we really were in a shocking plight. Horses staggered along the short distances between halts. Drivers were asleep on their mounts; gunners were flat out on wagons and limbers. Gardner was so tired he had to be held on a limber by an NCO. Why no one fell off and got left behind, hurt or killed I shall never know." [130]

Somehow Claud found reserves of energy to begin a letter to his mother on 29 March: *We have had a time of it in the past week. I've never known anything to equal it in all my life. It wasn't so much the fighting that has been so tiring but the continual movement and the lack of rest and sleep and not much food. Two days ago we were just about finished, men and horses, but we are stationery now at any rate for the time being and two days of comparative ease has put us back on our feet. I must say that three days ago I was nearly done in. Five days with only three hours sleep is a bit too much even for me who am pretty tough. When one adds to this some fairly heavy scrapping and a great deal of risk on continually finding the Hun almost round us, it is rather a strain to say the least.*

Claud had to break off at this point as the brigade received orders to move on. On 4 April he continued, *since then [the 29th] we have been marching and marching and now we have come to rest in a little village behind the line, where we are very comfortable. On the whole I think the brigade has come very well out of this show. Two or three times the Hun has nearly got us but we have all our guns and wagons intact and we have lost very little equipment. Of course men and horses are all tired but we have had practically no sickness amongst the men and, except for a good many shell wounds, very little wrong with the horses. I am sure the situation is much less acute than it was a week ago. I think the Hun has shot his bolt and we have him held and nowhere has he succeeded in breaking our line. I must say the Huns are marvellous and have run the offensive in a way that one cannot fail to admire. What a pity we couldn't do the same when we got our opening at Cambrai.*

---

[130] Carr, ibid p.118

The brigade marched southwards and then north west to avoid the German division which, having failed to take Arras, was now mounting an all out assault on Amiens with no more success. For the most part the days were again fine and warm, the countryside beautiful, châteaux, farms and villages untouched by war, the fruit trees in blossom. In one village they were the first British troops the people had seen. On the night of Easter Sunday they were billeted at Neuville and the hamlets of Wariville and Lorteil. The villagers welcomed them. Claud slept that night in a comfortable bed in a large farmhouse and had a much needed bath. The brigade rested there for the following day. Claud spent the morning sitting in the garden. The fine weather returned after a night of thunder and tropical rain. On 2 April they marched to Francastel, resting there for the night before a long 25 mile march to Morvillers-St Saturnin, the collection area where units arriving from the battle were being refitted. They stayed there for four days. During that time 17 German divisions made a mass attack towards Amiens and were beaten back, very largely as a result of the intense fire of the guns.

On 5 April Ludendorff admitted defeat. Operation 'Michael', the great offensive that would end the war, had failed. *Georgette* was no more successful. In sixteen days the British losses were far worse than Passchendaele. The 36th (Ulster) Division had been decimated. Each brigade had lost one of its battalions, killed or taken prisoner in the first two days, when the redoubt in the Forward Zone had been overrun. The Germans had lost at least as many. Furthermore, the majority of their losses were the highly trained storm-troopers, junior officers and NCOs, the leaders they could least afford to lose. Their loss was to affect the German army for the rest of the war.

The troops refitting at Poix-de-Picardie, the remnants of Fifth Army, were not drawn into the Amiens battle. About a fortnight's mail caught up with them, including a bundle of back numbers of Claud's *Times*. During the retreat they had had virtually no news of what was happening on other parts of the front. Now they were able to put the whole battle in context. The news from the Ypres salient was disturbing. In a new offensive the Germans had overwhelmed a Portuguese division. Armentières and Estaires, ten miles to the west had fallen. Claud took the opportunity to write another letter on 9 April, *the last three weeks seem like a colossal nightmare. I can hardly believe we have been through it all. We certainly had some hard times but the brigade kept well together.*

All the batteries did uncommonly well and I am very pleased with them. We are getting little news of the big battle here, but from all accounts the Hun is now well held and is taking tremendous casualties. He had committed himself to this final attempt to knock us out. If he fails he will be done for as he will have no men left to fight with. We, on the other hand, with the vast American resources to draw on, are getting stronger every day. I really do believe that this is going to be the end of the war, and I shall be surprised if we have to do another winter out here.

Whilst the batteries were watering their horses in Movillers, a convoy of staff cars had driven by containing Haig, the C-in-C, Lloyd George, the Prime Minister and Sir Henry Wilson, the newly appointed CIGS (and probably Winston Churchill, Minister for Munitions and Clemenceau, the French Prime Minister who were travelling with them, though Claud does not mention them by name, only as "etc").[131] On 26 March at the town hall at Doullens they had held a conference with a French delegation, led by the French President Poincaré and Marshal Petain, their C-in-C. The outcome was that both sides agreed that General Foch should be appointed to co-ordinate the Allied armies on the Western Front. Ultimately the appointment made little difference, but for the first time since the war began there was one overall commander.

On 11 April, 153rd Brigade marched to Renancourt, a suburb of Amiens to await the train that would take them north to Poperinghe. Amiens had suffered terribly from the German artillery and air raids and the civilian population had gone. A heavy air raid took place on the last morning, causing considerable damage and casualties. Some of the bombs fell not far from A Battery. On 14 April the brigade entrained at St Roch station. B Battery had almost completed loading when the station came under fire from heavy guns, scoring several direct hits on the train. Seven members of the battery were wounded, three of them seriously and five civilians were killed, including two women and two Australians. By the time the dead horses and debris had been cleared and the damaged railway wagons replaced, the train left for Poperinghe at 7.30 pm, five and a half hours later.

---

[131] The company commander of a weary retreating Middlesex company recalled how Churchill had stopped to talk to them and introduced him to Clemencau. "I tackled one of the British officers about a smoke. He emptied his cigarette case for me and Churchill gave us some fine cigars". Brown, ibid p.302.

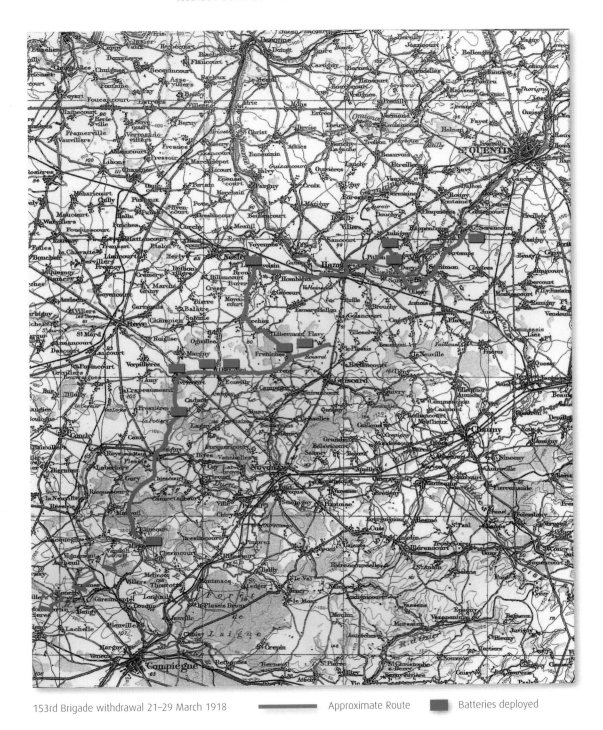

153rd Brigade withdrawal 21–29 March 1918 ━━━━━ Approximate Route ▮ Batteries deployed

Chapter 12   FROM *GEORGETTE* TO THE LAST HUNDRED DAYS

36th (Ulster) Division had just four days to reorganise between the arrival of the last train from the south and deployment into the line in the northeast of the salient at Poelcappelle. During these four days reinforcements flooded in from Britain to replace the desperately heavy casualties suffered in the March retreat. The majority of these reinforcements were 19 year old youths with far from adequate training. "In some cases almost before they knew their officers, they were put to the severest test and were to emerge with quite astonishing credit." [132]

On 9 April, the day after the division returned to the line, Ludendorff opened a new offensive, *Georgette,* with 17 divisions, the spearhead directed against the Portuguese division. The Portuguese broke, allowing the Germans to cross the Lys. On the first day they advanced on a front ten miles wide and five miles deep, heading for the vital railway junction at Hazebrouck. It was territory that had not been fought over up to that time – farm land where the farmers, believing themselves safe, had continued to work their farms. If the Germans could maintain that rate of advance, they could be in the Channel ports within a week. They were desperate days. On 11 April, the day after Armentieres fell, Haig issued his dramatic "backs to the wall" order of the day.

---

[132]   Falls, ibid p.233

Faced with the danger that they could be out-flanked, Passchendaele and Poelcappelle had to be abandoned. On 15 April, 36th Division, less 108th Brigade which had been redeployed in II Corps reserve, withdrew to a new line with its right flank just in front of Weiltje and its headquarters dug into the bank of the Ypres Canal. The detached brigade, 108th Brigade, now under command of 9th (Scottish) Division, was drawn into fierce fighting in the Messines area. On 17 April it withdrew behind Mount Kemmel, where it was relieved by French divisions sent up from the south, returning to its own division on 19 April. For the second time in a month the brigade had suffered heavy losses.

Meanwhile Claud's 153rd Brigade arrived at Poperinghe on the evening of 15 April, having travelled up by train from Amiens. There was to be no respite. They marched through the night in miserable conditions of wind and rain to establish wagon lines between Abeele and Mont des Cats, with brigade headquarters in the abbey. Having retired to bed at 3.30 am, Claud was up and out at 5.15 am to select gun positions at Berthen, a village he knew well, as he had been billeted there with 41st Division staff in July 1917. The house still stood but had been very badly damaged. Even as he watched he saw four shells fall into it. The gun positions covered a line from in front of St Jans Cappel to just behind Meteren. By 10 am the guns were in action putting down harassing fire on Bailleul and the aerodrome, firing barrages that effectively stopped the enemy's attempt to break through. There was an appreciable fall of snow that night, a sharp contrast to the mild days of the March retreat.

The next day was quiet from the brigade's point of view as the Germans changed direction, thrusting northwards from the area of Neuve Eglise, with Mont Kemmel as their objective. The brigade was given orders to fire 60 rounds per battery in each hour on Bailleul.[133] To Claud it seemed a sheer waste of ammunition. The guns were having to fire at near the limit of their range, placing a severe strain

---

[133] In January 1917 a number of old Marlburians gathered for a college dinner in Bailleul. In 2012, 50 descendants and family members of the original diners, among them Claud's grandson Tony, held a commemorative dinner in Bailleul provided by the catering students at Sainte Marie Vocational School, serving the identical six course menu of 95 years ago. The old friendly town had long since been destroyed, as completely as Ypres, not least in a bombardment in April 1915 in which Claud's brigade took part.

on the recuperation system that enabled the gun barrels to recoil to the firing positions between each round. By now the condition of the 18 pounders throughout the artillery was causing grave concern. Many of the carriages were badly worn and beyond repair.

A reluctant General Petain agreed at last to release some of his formations to the aid of the British, the French taking over the defence of Mont Kemmel from IX Corps. On 24 April seven German divisions succeeded in taking the hill, but were forced to retire by a combined French and British force at Locre on the other side of the hill. Ludendorff tried one more assault against the whole southern side of the British salient from Meteren to Zillebeke. The attack failed, achieving nothing. Next day Ludendorff called off *Georgette*. The casualties on both sides were staggering. In the six weeks since the launching of Operation 'Michael', the British had lost 240,000, the Germans 348,000.

Meanwhile, on 23 April, having handed over its gun positions to the French, the brigade came out of action and marched to Hamhoek north of Poperinghe where it rested for a day. Claud took the opportunity of cadging lifts to Dickebusch to visit his brother's grave. Ken had been much in his mind, for it was near Berthen that he had seen him for the last time, on the evening before he was killed. He found the wooden cross and grave *most neat and orderly and the cemetery very well kept*. In Poperinghe Claud had a narrow escape when a shell hit a house up the street, breaking the shop window he was looking in and peppering his back with fragments of brick.

On 25 April 153rd Brigade rejoined its parent division, a month after they had gone their separate ways in the last days of the March retreat, though for the next month it was not in support of the division. Instead it was deployed in the general area of Brielen, the batteries spanning the Ypres canal and half a mile north of St Jean, where they had been deployed for the opening of the Passchendaele battle in 1917. Its role was to cover the battalions' withdrawal to the west of the Steenbeck, north east of Ypres. Brigade headquarters was dug into the canal banks at C25d, opposite Nordhofwijk, with one gun position 700 yards to the west beside the old railway line. The war diary records that the brigade's task up to the end of the month was "brisk harassing fire on all tracks, roads and likely places of assembly." By night concentrations were brought down on all pillboxes and farms known to be occupied by the enemy, including Rat (C24a) and Bossaert Farms (C23b).

Though there was little infantry fighting in May on Second Army front, there was an ongoing artillery duel with both sides concentrating on the other's gun positions and using their heavy guns to straff wagon lines and rear areas. Aircraft were used to attack lines of communication and depots in the rear. The German gunners had learnt from the British the importance of counter battery fire, concentrating on individual positions rather than blanketing the whole area. The British adopted the tactics of dispersing individual sections and deploying single guns just behind the infantry to engage individual targets and then retire. One section carried out a highly successful shoot against a howitzer battery. A dump of shells and three dumps of charges were blown up, another two set on fire and three gun pits damaged extensively.

Claud was concerned about the increasing number of instances of shells falling on to own troops. A 6 inch howitzer shell nearly hit the brigade headquarters dugout. Possibly the cause was that barrels were becoming worn. They could be replaced but obviously only when the batteries were in a rest area. By the end of the war 99,300,000 18 pounder shells had been expended on the Western Front. [134]

The war diary records that May was devoted to "counter preparations and harassing fire on all targets likely to annoy the enemy and on likely places of assembly. Several gas concentrations fired." An entry on 5 June records an unsuccessful attack on a "wireless" plane by an enemy formation.[135]

All the batteries sustained casualties, both on the guns and in the wagon lines where the horses in particular suffered. In all five men were killed and six wounded. C Battery was heavily straffed, losing

---

[134] *British Artillery 1914-1919*, Dale Clark.

[135] This is the first mention of the brigade having wireless communications with an airborne observer correcting the fire of the batteries. Wireless had begun to be issued to brigades to enable them to talk to their batteries before the March retreat, but at first there were very few. A wireless would have been a godsend to Claud trying to keep in touch with his batteries.

three men killed, including an officer and a sergeant. On the same day another officer was wounded at an OP. Claud was dining with D Battery when the gun position came under heavy fire, 300 5.9 shells falling in the general area. The dinner went on uninterrupted, though the mess hut was peppered with shrapnel; an officer's coat hanging on a peg was punctured with splinters.

The May days were fine and warm, even hot. For three days the temperature had reached 80° Fahrenheit. The dugout was *extremely fuggy and frowsty and the rats and mosquitoes are awful*. Now there was a new hazard, the Spanish 'flu pandemic, believed to have been brought into Europe by the American units, which then infected both sides. The Allies, better fed and clothed, generally recovered quickly. The Germans, with their poor diet as a result of the sea blockade and with inferior clothing and boots, were more heavily afflicted.

In May Ludendorff launched his final offensive against the French and three British divisions which had been sent to what was expected to be a quiet area, having been badly mauled in the March retreat. The Allied front collapsed. The Germans reached the Marne after a spectacular advance and were within 60 miles of Paris. They were halted mainly by the 3rd American Division newly arrived from the United States, but also in some measure by the ravages of the 'flu.[136]

Nugent relinquished command, in May, of the 36th division which he had commanded since its arrival in France in 1915. He was posted to India, eventually to take over command of the Meerut Division, the division which Claud had served with in 1914. Claud shed no tears over Nugent's departure, for he regarded him as *a most unpleasant man*. He had been shot and taken prisoner in the Boer War and his ill-temper was exacerbated by the fact that the bullet was still lodged in his back, causing him constant pain. He was notorious for the number of commanding officers whom he had sacked. Nugent's replacement, General Clifford Coffin VC DSO, was a very different character. A former sapper, he had won his Victoria Cross for great bravery at Ypres. He soon visited the brigade, going round the batteries with Claud. *He seemed very pleased*, he told his mother in his next letter. *He's a friendly looking old bird, badly dressed and the most*

---

[136] A characteristic of the influenza was that those who caught it might die within 24 hours. 40 million people died world wide, far more than the total casualties of the war.

atrociously fitting breeches and gaiters. You would never take him for a VC hero. He's a nice old boy though and a welcome change from his predecessor.

On 7 June the 36th Division was withdrawn for seven weeks into a rest area between Houtkerque and Proven. It was relieved by the 12th Belgium Division, the batteries of their divisional artillery taking over 153rd Brigade's gun position one section at a time. Two of their artillery officers, *both delightful*, stayed in the brigade mess, whilst Claud took their CRA and group commander round the brigade area. Sadly one of their officers was killed before they had taken over.

The camp was a great success. The rest area chosen had suffered comparatively little from the destruction of war. At last the troops could look over green fields, see trees in full summer foliage and breathe fresh untainted air after the fetid atmosphere of the dugouts. The sleeping accommodation was in tents, the feeding in mess huts. For Claud's brigade it was an opportunity to carry out some badly needed training of young soldiers. It was a time for making up deficiencies in clothing and equipment, repairing harnesses. Above all it was time for nights of unbroken sleep.

The officers played rugby and polo; the men had inter-battery and brigade tournaments, running and boxing. There were brigade and divisional sports, the latter organised by Paul Petrie.[137] Visitors were inveigled into taking part in a three furlong mule race, bareback, without stirrups or whips.

Claud arranged a visit to the ordnance depot in Calais where material salvaged from the battlefield was reconstituted by a mixed labour force of local girls, German prisoners of war, Chinese and black South Africans. The boot repair shop was particularly interesting. Dirty old boots were made as good as new. From those that were too far gone, the soles were removed, mixed with sawdust and used as fuel, whilst the uppers were cut up to make boot laces. But the gunners were most interested in the shop where the French girls worked.

Many occupants of the camps were struck down by the 'flu bug, including Claud, but *after a day in bed I soon got better. It's extremely*

---

[137] Petrie was my uncle Paul, married to my mother's sister. See Chapter 5.

160

unpleasant whilst it lasts. One gets a high temperature, an awful head and pains all over. I felt very sorry for myself for 2 or 3 days but now I am as right as rain. He played rugby and ended up stiff and bruised. *The ground was hard and I was soft.*

The final event was a highly successful divisional horse show held on Proven aerodrome. *It really was a splendid affair and the turn-out of some of the competitors was simply marvellous. The jumping too was worth going a long way to see. It included an inter-divisional competition in which there were 11 entries including 4 Belgian teams. The latter were most awfully good and put our fellows completely in the shade.* One of the Belgians had ridden in the Olympic Games.

"Those seven weeks as a prelude to what was to come, were of inestimable worth", Falls wrote. "After long dreary months of trench warfare, the men had lost not only their physical agility, their powers to march and run but their mental powers as well. A spell such as this gave them not only new strength but also new heart, new spirit, new hope. When the division next entered the line, it was once again a fine fighting force." [138]

Refreshed, the recruits trained, the division returned to the line between Meteren and St Jans Cappel, covering the north west corner of the deep but now precarious salient which the Germans had created with the failure of *Georgette*. 153rd Artillery Brigade, now reinforced by 408, 409 and later 410 Batteries of 96th Army Field Artillery Brigade, the whole redesignated as the 'Potter Group', took over the positions vacated by the 4th French Division. *HQ in dugouts. Not very good, limited accommodation. Flies awful.* OPs were deployed on Mont Noir and Mont des Cats, looking down on the German battalions as they began to withdraw.

On 8 August Fourth Army, composed of a British corps and the Canadian and Australian corps, carried out an attack at Villers-Bretonneux on the axis of the Amiens-Roye road, supported by 2,000 field and heavy guns, 630 tanks and 800 aircraft. By evening they had advanced eight miles. Ludendorff was quoted as saying "It was the blackest day for the German army in the war." It was the beginning of the last 100 days.

---

[138] Falls, ibid p.246

All through the second half of August and most of September the three divisions of II Corps, 31st, 36th and 9th (Scottish), followed up the German withdrawal. Bailleul fell and then Neuve Eglise. All across the country to the east as far back as the Lys, great fires lit the night sky, accompanied by heavy explosions as the Germans destroyed ammunition dumps and defences. They fought tenaciously, carrying out a skilful withdrawal. Well-sighted machine guns covered the approaches to each hamlet, farm and hilltop. Heavy guns engaged the British gun positions, making indiscriminate use of gas. Several times shells fell a few yards from Claud. The farm at D Battery went up in a sheet of flames, setting off dumps of shells and charges, exploding for an hour. Claud had been to 108th Infantry Brigade to talk to General Vaughan, the brigade commander. On the way back he was caught in a bombardment of HE and gas shells. He pulled on his gas mask just in time, going back to his brigade *full of sneezes and feeling a bit sick and sorry*. One 5.9 shell had fallen very close to him. As the battalions pushed on, the batteries deployed to provide continuous cover. Claud was fully occupied going forward with his BCs to select new gun positions and OPs. By the last week of September he had moved his headquarters six times. On occasions sections or a single gun were deployed forward to keep up with the infantry.

Both sides were using gas (diphosgene, lachrymatory and mustard). One battery of 173rd Brigade was put out of action completely and had to be withdrawn temporarily. Claud had set up his headquarters in an old stable and pigsty 2,400 yards south east of Danoutre (T2c). When it came under heavy fire from a 5.9, they had to shelter behind the farm and wear their gas masks long into the night.

The next headquarters location, 400 yards to the east, seemed ideal, a farm with deep cellars. However, when a warning was circulated that the enemy was leaving delayed action mines in dugouts and locations likely to be used by the British, Claud moved his men out that night. Thereafter they slept in rough temporary shelters and bivouacs (known then, as now, as 'bivvies'). Perversely the weather broke, with five days of incessant rain, hail and gales.

On 8 September the 'Potter Group' was reconstituted with the two divisional artillery brigades less B Battery of 173rd Brigade, which was still recovering from the gas attack. Claud set up his group headquarters with HQ 107th Infantry Brigade behind Neuve Eglise. By now the front ran from Gooseberry Farm (U7b) to Hyde Park Corner in Ploegstreet Wood (U19b). Five days later Claud lost one of his battery commanders, Reid of B Battery, killed when a 5.9 shell landed on his dugout.

From mid August through September the Germans were falling back before the onslaught of almost simultaneous offensives launched by the British, French and Americans. In Palestine, Allenby was well on the way to overwhelming the Turks. The Bulgarians were on the run in Macedonia. The Austrians' final attack in Northern Italy had failed. Though to the participants it may not have seemed like it, the war was drawing to a close.

In comparison the operations of the Second Army in the north, though effective, had been less spectacular. Now it was time for it to take its place in the final battle. Four British corps, the Belgian corps and a French division all under the supreme command of the King of the Belgians, would drive eastwards from Ypres. Preliminary moves were to be carried out in the greatest secrecy.

On 18 September Claud visited the headquarters of the Belgian corps and II Corps. At the latter he met and was briefed about his brigade's part in the coming battle by the GOC RA, General Kirby. He called in at headquarters 9th (Scottish) Division and met the CRA, General Wainwright. The brigade was to supplement the 9th Divisional Artillery in the preliminary barrage. On his way home he had dinner with General Brock, who had commanded the 36th Divisional Artillery since its arrival in France two and a half years ago. He was now to take over command of 107th Infantry Brigade. He was, Claud told his mother, a 'difficile' *person, very strict and a bit of a martinet, but most awfully efficient and looked after all our interests very well.* Until such time as a replacement was appointed, Claud was to act as CRA.[139] By the time Claud caught up with his headquarters, the brigade had withdrawn from the battle zone to wagon lines around Croix de Poperinghe (M32b).

[139] The vacancy in 107th Brigade arose when the previous commander, General Thorpe, had been shot and wounded by one of his own soldiers.

As the units assembled for the coming battle, all movement was to take place at night. On a brightly moonlit night, to the accompaniment of the sounds of air raids somewhere to the rear, probably Dunkirk and Calais, the brigade marched to a billeting area around Haandekot, north of Watou. Claud was allocated a billet in a farm with a soft bed and clean sheets. *It's grand to be able to sleep in pyjamas, get up when you feel inclined and above all no wretched telephone ringing through the night.* Next day, whilst the brigade remained at rest, he and his BCs drove in a lorry to Brielen in the north west suburb of Ypres to recce the positions for their guns. An officer and 12 men per battery were sent forward to secure these positions.

On 25 September Claud and his brigade major visited the corps headquarters at Cassel. *I am now an Acting CRA.* It was the last entry he was to make in the diary that he had maintained since 20 September 1914, the day he was sailing through the Channel on the troop ship *Gloucester Castle*.[140] On 26 September the guns moved into position. The limber gunners were left overnight to keep watch on them until the detachments arrived the following day. Brigade headquarters deployed in the ramparts that surround Ypres to this day.

Second Army's offensive began on 28 September. At the outset it was a resounding success. Zero hour was at 5.30 am, the barrage began at 4.55 am, with 153rd Brigade firing in support of 9th Division of the left of the II Corps front. By 6.40 am an excited FOO in Potijze was reporting that the enemy was "running like hell", with our infantry following up close behind the barrage. The Germans put up no resistance. At 10.40 am the brigade major of 9th Divisional Artillery reported that his division had advanced as far as Broodseinde crossroads (D23c). By the end of the day the division had advanced 6,000 yards and the 8th Belgian Division had taken Zonnebeke.

Once the creeping barrage had ceased, the batteries were to move forward and take up positions along Cambridge Road. However, the guns were held up by the density of the traffic and the condition of the roads, made worse by incessant rain. By the time the brigade

---

[140]   From here on this account is based on the brigade war diary held in the National Archives at Kew.

headquarters had reached Potijze Château, the speed of the battalions' advance had been so rapid that they were out of the range of the 18 pounders. They were ordered to move on and take up positions east of Frenzenberg ridge, with the headquarters in the village, but it was after dusk before they were in position. That night German bombers carried out heavy air attacks on the approaches to the front line, causing casualties in the batteries.

The following day, 29 September, 36th Division, which had been in corps reserve, was committed to the battle. 153rd Brigade reverted to supporting its own division, but because of the hazards of moving forward on roads in a shocking condition, the batteries were unable to provide fire support until the following day. Incessant rain had made movement extremely difficult not only for the guns but also for the ammunition column. By evening Dadizeele and Vijwegen had fallen to 9th and 36th Divisions.

By 30 September the picture was changing. German resistance was stiffening along the line of the main road from Menin to Roulers, with its high embankments providing both observation and a screen to movement on the far side, whilst Hill 41, 60 feet high, dominated the approaches. Attempts to take the hill on 29 September had failed. Another attempt was made on 1 October. The brigade fired a barrage in support and two batteries of 6 inch howitzers joined in at long range. Again the attack failed, beaten back by machine guns hidden behind hedges. By now the battlefield had moved beyond the devastated countryside of the Ypres salient. The Germans had brought up fresh troops and artillery. On 2 October, the last day of the fourth Battle of Ypres, Dadizeele came under a heavy barrage but the following German counter attack failed.[141]

HQ 153rd Brigade had moved into a concrete dugout recently vacated by the Germans, built into the bank of a road running north west 800 yards from Terhand (K14a), shown on a trench map as part of the third German defence line covering the Passchendaele front. Somehow Claud found time to write to his mother, apologising

---

[141] Hill 41 was not finally overrun until 14 October, the first phase in a II Corps operation based around 36th Division, with the divisional artillery supported by the corps 'heavies'. The operation led to the capture of Coutrai.

The site of the dugout and its possible entrance. On a fine autimn day in 2009, armed with the original map sheet, it was a simple matter to find the site, taking the road from Beclaere to Terhand. The dugout had been built into an embankment opposite a farm. Now covered by long grass, there was no sign of it, though this concrete cover at one end may have protected the entrance.

for writing on a message pad left behind by a German signaller, *I have only one blanket and what I stand up in, such luxuries as writing paper not to be had. Lucky to have any paper at all. Our show went awfully well. Hun was surprised and overwhelmed. We got a lot of prisoners and guns with very little loss. Weather has been against us. Can't imagine anything more horrible than yesterday and the day before. Pelted with rain with very icy cold strong wind and everyone was pretty miserable. At the end of the first day, in which our Brigade was attached to another Division, we rejoined our own Division and I was called to act as CRA, so I am now commanding eight batteries of artillery, some heavies and the ammunition column. Very interesting work and very good experience. I was lucky to find myself acting as CRA during a battle. One usually associates it with a period of great comfort, a good mess and billet and a car. However, there is none of that now, as we are at advanced divisional headquarters in this dugout with the minimum of comfort.* The letter was dated 3 October, the last letter he was to write to his mother from the battlefield.

On the morning of 5 October the brigade war diary reported that the enemy artillery had become far more active. Shells had fallen on A battery wagon lines and several horses had been killed. At about

9 pm a shell landed right on top of the brigade headquarters mess dugout.[142] Of the five occupants, Claud was the only one to survive.[143] His brigade major, Franklyn, visited him at the advanced dressing station in Potijze Chateau. That evening Franklyn wrote to Claud's mother. He told her that her son had had a miraculous escape. The doctor had confirmed that it was quite a small wound, but the official War Office telegram referred to "a severe gunshot wound".

The journey by stretcher bearer and ambulance over roads in a shocking state and jam-packed with traffic moving forward had taken eight hours and had been very uncomfortable. At one point the ambulance had been bogged down in a ditch.[144] His leg had not been put in a splint and by the time he had reached the casualty clearing station it had swollen up like a balloon. From the CCS he was evacuated by hospital train to the 5th Anglo-American Red Cross hospital at Wimereux on the coast four miles north of Le Havre. There were, he now discovered, six holes in his leg, some of them of a size about half way between a golf ball and a cricket ball. As the only one of her three sons left, he was worried about how he was going to support his mother. Despite the fact that at the time he was hit he had been a lieutenant colonel and acting as CRA, a brigadier's post that he must have had a fair chance of retaining, from now on he would be paid in his substantive rank of major, a reduction to about half of his income. On 18 October he was brought back to England and admitted to the King Edward VII Hospital for Officers, five minutes walk from Victoria Station, regarded as the best officers' hospital in the country. A week after the Armistice, since there were

---

[142] It is possible that the explosion was caused not by a shell but by a delayed action mine left behind by the previous occupants. There is no trace of a shell crater on top of the dugout.

[143] The four dead are buried in Potijze War Cemetery on the outskirts of Ypres. Their graves are in a separate group at the head of all the others, the last dead to be buried there.

[144] Nineteen years later Claud, by then retired, received a letter from a Lieutenant Learmouth with an address in Cologne, dated 1 January 1937, reminding him that it was he who had supervised the unditching of the ambulance. Claud had written from the hospital to thank him. Apparently at that time he had been a German prisoner of war, a Jew named Levi, who had now changed his name by Deed Poll to Learmouth "owing to events here in Germany". Perhaps he had hoped that Claud could help him to leave Germany and escape the pogrom, but by that time Claud was settled in Northern Ireland. There is nothing to show whether the correspondence continued.

no more casualties arriving from France, the remaining patients were moved to Lady Wernher's Hospital for wounded officers in a wing of her great house, Luton Hoo.

Claud made such good progress there that by December he was able to move around on crutches. An appointment had been made for him to go up to London for a final course of massage before being discharged from hospital. However, on 7 December he slipped, falling full length in a stone passage, breaking his leg, the leg with the wounds. It was a bitter disappointment. He had planned to spend Christmas in Ilkley and Devon. Instead he spent it in bed, flat on his back again, listening to the choir of Luton Parish Church singing carols in the chapel downstairs. He had one consolation. In the New Years Honours he had been appointed a Companion of the Order of St Michael and St George, a rare award for a substantive major.

It was a sad day when the hospital closed down at the end of February 1919 and he was moved to a convalescent home in Berkhamstead, where all the other inmates were boisterous subalterns. *I was so absolutely happy there* [in Luton Hoo], he told his mother. *I was awfully sorry to say goodbye to the Matron who had become a very dear friend of mine. I can't tell you how good she was to me. I miss her most awfully. In fact I am feeling very lonely and depressed.* After four years of war, the love and gentleness and care of a woman must have had a profound effect on him. He had fallen in love.[145]

---

[145] *Falling Blossom*, a biography of Brigadier General Hart-Synott, who had lost both his legs at Arras in May 1918, was a patient at Luton Hoo at the same time as Claud, though neither mentions the other. The book gives a description of the house "originally designed by Richard Adam, had been bought by the diamond merchant Sir Julius Wernher in 1903 and extensively altered. The architect responsible for the Ritz redecorated the interior with ornate panelling and fireplaces, gilded ribbons and festoons to provide a setting for Sir Julius's art collection. Wernher died in 1913, leaving an immense fortune, and his widow made her contribution to the war effort by lending her house as a convalescent home. Lady Wernher, a society beauty known as 'Birdie' who had lost her youngest son during the Somme, took a personal interest in the convalescents and came to visit". The book includes a sketch by Hart-Synott of his room with its own bathroom and dressing room. The family estate Ballymoyer in South Armagh is now a National Trust property. Sadly the house there has been demolished in recent years. *Falling Blossom*, Peter Pagnamenta and Momoko Williams.

Claud's last letter from the war, written on a German message pad.

Station _____   Abteilung _____

angenommen am / 19 ___ Uhr ___ Min. vorm. / nachm. durch _____
aufgenommen am / 19 ___ Uhr ___ Min. vorm. / nachm. durch _____ von _____
befördert am / 19 ___ Uhr ___ Min. vorm. / nachm. durch _____ an _____

Fern= Licht= Funk= **Spruch** Nr. _____ aus _____

Dienstliche Zusätze:

Absender:	ᵗᵉ Meldg.	Ort	Dat.	Zeit
	Abgegangen			
	Angekommen			

An

Chapter 13 AFTERMATH

In 1919 Claud was declared fit for duty and was attached to a reserve brigade. In the following year he was posted to 52nd Lowland Division in a major's appointment. He met and married Anne Tinn, widow of a lieutenant in the Highland Light Infantry. He had died of pneumonia seven months after their wedding, leaving the widow with a small son, Farquhar. She inherited her husband's estate, Kirkhill, in Colmonell, an Ayrshire village looking down on the beautiful glen of the Stinchar.

Within weeks of Claud's marriage to Anne, she too died, leaving him to bring up a child, now an orphan. Having survived the horrors of the war, Claud's hopes for a life of love and peace had been shattered. In July 1921 he was promoted to lieutenant colonel and given command of the 3rd Artillery Brigade, stationed in Cologne as part of the occupying force in the British Army of the Rhine (BAOR). He arranged for Mary Paton, one of the maids at Kirkhill, to come with him as nursemaid to little Farquhar. She stayed with the family, a much loved nanny, for the rest of her life.

Farquhar went on to have a somewhat troubled life as a schoolboy and a young man. He was interested in the stage and attended the Royal Academy of Dramatic Art but made nothing of it. He had inherited a small fortune from his parents. On a visit to Monte Carlo he met a beautiful ballet dancer, Nina Tarakanova. A White Russian, she had escaped from the Soviet Union at the time of the revolution in 1917 and settled in Paris. She began her career with Diaghilev's ballet, where her vivacious aura soon won her solo parts. In 1938, when they were married, she was at the peak of her career during a season at Drury Lane. The marriage, however, did not last long. When war was declared in 1939, Farquhar joined the RAF Volunteer Reserve as a pilot officer, flying Lancasters out of Witchford in Cambridgeshire, a station that suffered the greatest number of losses in the whole of Bomber Command. He was killed in January 1944, shot down over Berlin, dying gallantly, remaining at the controls to give his crew members time to escape.

In August 1922 Claud married Gwen Fell of Ilkley, Yorkshire. She was the younger sister of Eileen Petrie.[146] After a honeymoon in Skye, they settled down in a house on Rheinufer Strasse in Cologne. The house survived the war and was still standing in the 1960s. The *Deutsch Mark* had collapsed and life was hard for the conquered Germans, but Claud and Gwen had a good life, the newly married couple much in demand for dinner parties, concerts, nights at the opera and holidays in the Ahr valley.

In the following March Claud and Gwen drove to Flanders to visit the battlefields. It was a fraught journey. The condition of the roads varied between new *pavé* to the appalling potholes of the Menin-Ypres road, the stretch from Gheluvelt onwards almost impassable. Not surprisingly they had punctures, first one, and then another, then a third. As a result of some mechanical fault that was never rectified despite the efforts of several garages *en route*, the car baulked at climbing hills. On one particularly steep hill they had to abandon it three quarters way up, carry their luggage to the top and then walk back to the car, which, with a lighter load, managed to struggle up the rest of the way.

In Ypres they stayed in 'Skindles', an off-shoot of the famous officers' club in Poperinghe. It was only half finished, very bare and primitive and not very clean. Apart from the Cathedral, the Cloth Hall and the moat outside the Menin Gate, there was little left of the town that Claud could recognise, but when heavy rain churned up the mud it was *just typical of the good old wartime Wipers.*

---

[146] See Chapter 5

At Potijze War Cemetery Claud and Gwen visited the graves of the four officers killed in the dugout when Claud had been wounded. He found his headquarters dugout in the bank of the Comines canal, long since fallen in, and some of his gun positions, but the land had been so extensively restored that it was difficult to pinpoint the exact locations. All the ruined houses and farms had been rebuilt on the same sites, trenches and shell holes filled in, barbed wire removed, crops and pastures cultivated where 'No Man's Land' had been. At St Eloi there were some traces of the trenches of both sides, huge heaps of barbed wire, pieces of equipment, stick bombs and human bones. On the fields of Passchendaele a few tanks were rusting away. They drove into France, visiting Le Touret where Claud had his first battery position of the war. The elderly couple he had been billeted on in the village were still there and gave him a warm welcome. But when the French customs were bloody minded, demanding an exorbitant deposit on the car, they abandoned their battlefield tour and spent three happy days in Bruges, picnicking in the dunes and visiting the German U-Boat pens at Zeebrugge.

Claud retired in 1925 after a quarter of a century of army service. He said goodbye to his brigade in a special order of the day, dated four days before I was born. He bought the 'Mount', a house in a small village on the Nottingham-Lincolnshire border. It had changed little since the turn of the century, almost feudal in its hierarchy, with the squire Claud; the gentleman farmer Mr Butcher; the vicar Mr Dangerfield; the grocer Mr Bell; and the inn keeper. All village life revolved around them. It was at last a happy, tranquil time in that backwater, until Gwen contracted infantile paralysis. She made a good recovery, but was lame for the rest of her life. She died in 1972.

Claud commuted by train, a LNER express, to Leeds where he was a member of a firm of stockbrokers founded by his grandfather. The work was not much to his liking. When in 1930 one of his old friends in the 36th (Ulster) Division wrote to tell him that the post of bursar at Campbell College, Northern Ireland's leading public school, had become vacant and he might care to apply. He did so and was accepted. Claud and Gwen, and their three children, David, Helen and John, moved to Holywood, where they bought 'Abingdon', which became the family home.

'Abingdon', Holywood c.1915

Claud's administrative experience on two divisional staffs during the war made him an ideal choice. The headmaster was another ex-service officer, Colonel 'Duffy' Gibbon. They were a well matched pair, much loved and respected. The school had a fine reputation for providing officers for the services. On the outbreak of the Second World War the pupils were evacuated to the Northern Counties Hotel in Portrush. Claud and the family moved to Portstewart. Claud retired when the school came back to Belfast after the war, but he continued to work as secretary to Cabin Hill, the preparatory school, remaining in that post until his death on 29 January 1965, four months short of his 84th birthday. He is buried in Redburn Cemetery in Holywood.

Claud was President of the Holywood branch of the Royal British Legion from 1935 until his death. He was a regular church goer in Holywood Parish Church. The vicar, Canon Eric Barber, said of him that he was "the perfect Christian gentleman. He wore the white flower of a blameless life. It would be wrong to speak of any human character as perfect – but he was nearer than anyone I ever met. The 'Colonel', as we all knew him, leaves behind the fragrance of a blameless life. We shall not see his like again."

SPECIAL ORDER
by
LIEUT-COLONEL C.F. POTTER, C.M.G., D.S.O. R.A.
- - - - - - - - -

COLOGNE 30.6.1925.

In saying goodbye on terminating my 4 years Command
of the Royal Artillery of the Rhine Army, I wish to take
this opportunity of thanking every Officer, Warrant Office,
Non-commissioned officer and man for the loyal support
I have invariably received from all those whom it has been
my privelege to have under my Command.

I can confidently say that the reputation of the
Royal Artillery of the Rhine Army stands very high.
The discipline is excellent, the turn-out of Batteries in
general and of all ranks individually all that one could
wish for, whilst the excellent relationship between officers
W.Os, N.C.O's and men points to a very good "tone" throughout
the Artillery as a whole.

I wish all of you the very best of good fortune in
whatever sphere of life the future may have in store for you,
and I look forward to many renewals of the greatly valued
friendships I have made during my time in Cologne.

Lieut-Colonel, R.A.

Claud's
Special Order of the Day
30 June 1925

Bibliography

Blake, Robert (ed) *The Private Papers of Sir Douglas Haig, 1914-1919*, quoted by Brown *ibid*

Brown, Malcolm *The Imperial War Museum Book of the Western Front*. Pan Books, 2001

Carr, William *A Time to Leave the Ploughshares. A Gunner Remembers 1917-18*. London, Robert Hale, 1985

Clark, Dale *British Artillery 1914-1919*. Osprey, 2004

Corrigan, Gordon *Sepoys in the Trenches: The Indian Corps in the Western Front 1914-15*. Spellmount, 2006

Cooper, Jilly *Animals in War*. Transworld, 2004

Doyle, Sir Arthur Conan *A visit to Three Fronts June 1916*. Copied from Classic Literature Library web site

Farndale, General Sir Martin *History of the Royal Regiment of Artillery, Western Front 1914-1918*. Royal Artillery Institution, 1986

Falls, Cyril *The History of the 36th (Ulster) Division*. The Linenhall Press, 1922

Gibbs, Philip *The Battle of the Somme*. Heineman, 1917

Giles, John *The Ypres Salient, Then and Now*. Leo Cooper, 1970. Revised 1979 and republished by Picardy Publishing Ltd.

Hart, Liddell *History of the First World War*. Cassell and Co, 1930

Higgins, Sydney *The Golden Age of British Theatre (1880-1920)*

Holmes, Richard *Tommy: The British Soldier on the Western Front*. Harper Collins, 2004

Keegan, John *The First World War*. Random House, 1998

Mollo, Boris *The Indian Army*. Blandford Books, 1981

Moreno, Amanda and Truesdale, David *Angels and Heroes. The Story of a Machine Gunner with the Royal Irish Fusiliers August 1914 to April 1915, as recorded by Sergeant Hugh Wilson (Medaille Militaire)*, 2004

O'Sullivan, Mrs Denis, (ed) *Harry Butters RFA. 'An American Citizen'. Life and War Letters*. John Lane Co, 1918

Pagnamenta, Peter and Williams, Momoko *Falling Blossom: A British Officer's Enduring Love for a Japanese Woman*. Century, 2006

Palit. Maj Gen D K (ed) *History of the Regiment of Artillery, Indian Army*. Leo Cooper, 1972

Pile, General Sir Frederick *Ack-Ack: Britain's Defence against Air Attack during the Second World War*. Harrop, 1949

Simpson, Keith *The Old Contemptibles*. Allen & Unwin, 1930

Steel, Nigel and Hart, Peter *Passchendaele, The Sacrificial Ground*. Cassell & Co, 2000

Abbreviations	AA	Anti-aircraft
	AA & QMG	Assistant Adjutant and Quartermaster General
	ADMS	Assistant Director of Medical Services
	ADS	Advanced Dressing Station
	AEF	American Expeditionary Force
	APM	Assistant Provost Marshal
	BC	Battery Commander
	BEF	British Expeditionary Force
	BGRA	Brigadier General Royal Artillery
	BK	Battery Captain
	BSM	Battery Sergeant Major
	CCS	Casualty Clearing Station
	CIGS	Chief of the Imperial General Staff
	C-in-C	Commander-in-Chief
	CMG	Companion of the Order of St Michael and St George
	CO	Commanding Officer
	CRA	Commander Royal Artillery
	DF	Defensive Fire
	DSO	Distinguished Service Order
	FOO	Forward Observation Officer
	GHQ	General Headquarters
	GOC	General Officer Commanding
	HE	High Explosive
	HQ	Headquarters
	How	Howitzer
	MC	Military Cross
	Mg	Machine gun
	NCO	Non Commissioned Officer
	OC	Officer Commanding
	OP	Observation Post
	OR	Other rank
	OS	Observation Station
	RFA	Royal Field Artillery
	RFC	Royal Flying Corps
	TM	Trench Mortar

Biography

John Potter was born in 1925, the younger son of Lieutenant Colonel Claud Potter. In 1948 he married Cynthia Davison, by whom he had a son, Tony, and a daughter, Nicola.

John was educated at Marlborough College, Wiltshire. He served in Queen's University Belfast Officers' Training Corps. In 1944 he followed his father into the Royal Artillery. He served in India, the Suez Canal Zone and Germany. He retired with the rank of Major.

John joined the Ulster Defence Regiment in 1971, a year after it was formed. He was appointed Adjutant of the 3rd (County Down) Battalion, later becoming the Regimental Secretary. He served in the Regiment for 21 years until its merger with the Royal Irish Rangers in 1992. He is the author of *A Testimony to Courage*, the regimental history of the Ulster Defence Regiment. He was awarded MBE.

John was a trustee of the Northern Ireland War Memorial from 1984 to 2012. During his 28 years on the Board, he devoted much time to building up and managing a Home Front exhibition, which became the core of the new War Memorial gallery when the NIWM moved to its present premises in Talbot Street, Belfast in 2007.

John is the author of two monographs *The Belfast Blitz 1941* and *Passing Through*, the story of the US forces in Northern Ireland from 1942 to 1944. He is also the co-author with Murray Barnes of *The Twelve Mile Snipers*, the story of the 8th (Belfast) Heavy Anti-Aircraft Regiment, Royal Artillery (Supplementary Reserve) 1939-1945.